Carolyn Strong
Small Enterprise Marketing

Carolyn Strong

Small Enterprise Marketing

Eighteen Case Studies

DE GRUYTER

ISBN 978-3-11-075612-8
e-ISBN (PDF) 978-3-11-075614-2
e-ISBN (EPUB) 978-3-11-075623-4

Library of Congress Control Number: 2024935954

Bibliographic information published by the Deutsche Nationalbibliothek
The Deutsche Nationalbibliothek lists this publication in the Deutsche Nationalbibliografie;
detailed bibliographic data are available on the internet at http://dnb.dnb.de.

© 2024 Walter de Gruyter GmbH, Berlin/Boston
Cover image: bb-doll/iStock/Getty Images Plus
Typesetting: Integra Software Services Pvt. Ltd.

www.degruyter.com

Foreword

Entrepreneurship and entrepreneurial activity have gained increasing prominence in recent decades, particularly with a view to wealth creation and economic development. Seen broadly as the activity of setting up a business and taking on financial risks in the hope of profit (*Oxford Dictionary*), there has been much debate around defining entrepreneurship and an entrepreneur. Many of these stem from either the Schumpeterian or Kiznerian views. Schumpeter's view points to the entrepreneur's ability to create change due to their internal disposition, alluding to the entrepreneur's actions leading to 'creative destruction'. Alternatively, Kizner emphasised opportunity recognition, and the ability of entrepreneurs to use their existing information and knowledge to make something profitable through 'entrepreneurial alertness.'[1]

With changing economic times, entrepreneurship has become more prominent. Since the Industrial Revolution we have seen various waves of innovation that have influenced new developments in technology and new entrepreneurial opportunities. In the late 1700s water power created opportunities for the development of industry, while steam power and the development of railways in the mid-1800s facilitated trade and travel, as did developments in internal combustion engine, and later aviation, throughout the 1900s. More recently, the development of the internet has disrupted many industries, such as retail and media, leading to a new wave of businesses and entrepreneurial activity, with great potential in the development of Artificial Intelligence (AI) and the Internet of Things.

The development of the internet has seen the rapid emergence of a number of global technological companies, such as Apple, Amazon and Samsung. While these represent some of the largest businesses in the world, their origins stem from the vision of their entrepreneurs. They were once small startup businesses but have grown over time into the businesses that they are today. While these large global businesses often appear more prominent, we must also acknowledge the importance of small businesses.

Big isn't always beautiful, and small businesses are considered the backbone of many economies, often representing over 95% of all businesses in certain countries, and therefore important drivers of job creation and economic growth. Within this, the vast majority are usually micro-enterprises (with less than 10 employees), and typically just the entrepreneur as sole trader. While smaller businesses lack the resources, capabilities and financial capital of more established larger businesses, access to a global marketplace through the internet means that opportunities are more prominent than ever for small businesses to support growth, both domestically and internationally.

Strategically, countries often look to small businesses as a way of promoting economic development, placing an emphasis on supporting entrepreneurship over for-

---

1 Kirzner, I. M. (1973). *Competition and entrepreneurship*. University of Chicago Press.

https://doi.org/10.1515/9783110756142-202

eign investment. Differences can be seen around the world in national approaches towards entrepreneurship, including investment in innovation, the ease of setting up and operating a business and support available in the development and growth of a business. Entrepreneurship is often seen as a source of organic growth, and a way of creating new jobs and supporting the local economy. Consequently, entrepreneurship is becoming increasingly prominent within education, particularly at the university level, as a subject in its own right within business schools and also through business startup competitions open to all students. Indeed, universities are acknowledged as important actors within local entrepreneurial ecosystems and a source of spin-out businesses.

All businesses are different, and the entrepreneurial journeys of businesses differ according to a range of factors, including the sector in which they operate, the market conditions, the vision of the entrepreneur and even luck. Small businesses tend to possess fewer resources compared to larger businesses, and therefore become more vulnerable to challenging economic conditions. This was apparent during the COVID-19 pandemic, as many small businesses faced challenges due to lockdown restrictions, and many didn't have the resources, knowledge or capabilities to pivot towards online activity, or diversify their offering. That said, small businesses can also benefit from agility in adapting to new conditions as the decision-making process can often be simpler as it is only the owner-manager making decisions on the direction of the business.

Consequently, we can learn a great deal from the experiences of different businesses, and exploring case studies of businesses can tell us so much about what entrepreneurs have done to develop their business, which can lead to new ideas and new ways of thinking entrepreneurially. By considering a range of case studies, it is possible to see how new ideas have developed, and how the businesses have been influenced by the context of their location, sector and specific circumstances. Thus, the aim of this book in presenting various case studies on entrepreneurial businesses is valuable in highlighting the various ways in which entrepreneurship can develop, outlining notable examples of businesses, in a variety of settings, that have managed to leverage their resources, capabilities and knowledge to pursue growth.

This book presents a collection of case studies around three themes of businesses having a positive social impact, small family businesses and businesses that have a community and society benefit. The case studies draw on a range of examples of businesses from different settings, but which have an important place-specific focus.

The first section explores businesses that have a positive social impact, including a net-zero carbon office furniture business, an inclusive summer camp for children, a sustainable community-supported fishery, an ethically sourced specialty coffee company, an ethical luxury skincare company and a responsible fashion company. The second section explores community-focused businesses, notably a hotel, a fine dining restaurant, a circular economy furniture producer, a sustainable clothing brand, a sustainably focused football club and a sustainably foraged seaweed food business. The final section presents family businesses, including a gin company, a celebration cake business, a non-profit coffee shop, an experiential food business, a power distribution and infrastructure business and a woollen mill producing blankets and throws.

These case studies provide valuable learnings about these businesses, underlining the challenges and opportunities that small businesses face in the changing economic times. They present interesting and novel business ideas and show that businesses can have a significant societal impact in different settings, even with limited resources and challenging economic conditions. These learnings can help to inspire new businesses in the future.

Dr Robert Bowen

Acknowledgements

This case studies book would never have materialised without Steve Hardman and Maximillian Gessl of De Gruyter. We talked extensively about the idea of a case studies story telling book and created this text between us. I enjoyed working with you both, especially our online meetings when we talked about our family, our cats, our favourite Netflix series and laughed together. Thank you, Steve and Maximillian, I will miss working with you both.

Thank you to the chapter contributors Adam Mills, Christine Pitt and Anthony Samuel.

Thank you to the outstanding students Lisa Griffith, Brodi Parfitt and Lucie Collins who generated ideas about some of the case studies from a student perspective.

Thank you to the small business owners who gave me their time in various ways and shared their stories which allowed this book to happen.

Thank you also to Lucy Jarman (De Gruyter) who closed the book, scrutinising, sharpening, and polishing the final text.

https://doi.org/10.1515/9783110756142-203

Contents

Introduction

This book tells the stories of a selection of successful small business enterprises. It is not an account of financial success or brand share but a collection of narratives on the journeys made by inspiring, determined, innovative individuals who have applied their passion and skills to the creation of successful small businesses. These stories of diverse small businesses illustrate how success can be achieved through desire and determination. They include tales of entrepreneurs with a love of seaweed and a passion for fashion, as well as accounts of family survival.

The case studies tell compelling stories of personal achievement and business success and encourage the reader to find out more about the small business owners and their products. These small businesses present a challenge to the market equilibrium and create excitement and interest in their goods and strategies. While each enterprise is financially thriving and growing its market share, the case studies do not refer to finances, market share or profit.

The stories are about small, strong brands that are socially viable, well established and trustworthy. These brands have built relationships, and even friendships, with their customers. They form part of a range of businesses providing local training and employment (often for marginalised members of their community) and making a positive contribution to society. Across all the case studies, there is a recurring theme of not just making a profit; money is important but not always essential to drive, passion or motivation for success.

The case studies are divided into three themes: socially conscious small business enterprises, small business enterprises providing societal benefit and family-run small business enterprises. The case studies are collated from conversations, talks, presentations, interviews and secondary sources.[1]

I came across some of these entrepreneurs in my personal life. I met Eifion and Amanda when I spent weekends in Fishguard, West Wales, finding Melin Tregwynt by chance and chatting to the owners. I discovered the Pembrokeshire Beach Food Company during a COVID-19-travel-restricted family summer holiday in Freshwater West. I bought Gower Gin during lockdown and loved Sian and Andrew's approach to foraging for natural local ingredients and diversifying their distillery production to manufacture hand sanitiser for local healthcare providers. While on holiday in the Algarve, I observed Paulo running his family restaurant businesses. I worked with Mercedes Noam over 12 years ago when they were a young entrepreneur working in London; we reconnected during lockdown when I invited them to give a Zoom presentation to Cardiff Business School students from Costa Rica. I have long been aware of Antagrade Electrical, a family-run small business.

---

1 SREC reference: 799.

https://doi.org/10.1515/9783110756142-001

I met the other small business innovators through Cardiff Business School: Rype Office provides sustainable furniture; Greenstream Flooring CIC has supplied circular-economy flooring for building renovation and refurbishment projects; Manumit Coffee Roasters supplies slavery-free coffee for the staff and PhD student kitchen; The Goodwash Company, Modest Fashion London and Let Them See Cake have supported Cardiff Business School students through entrepreneurial, live-assessment business projects. Community leader Adrian Emmett was introduced to me by a colleague who was astounded by this small business owner's approach to bringing his small-town community together during the COVID-19 pandemic.

Adam Mills, Christine Pitt, Anthony Samuel and Robert Bowen. contributed four of the case studies, bringing their insightful perspectives to the book.

Small business enterprise can be likened to sand on the beach: the landscape changes every day depending on the tide; it can be predicted to some extent, but other uncontrollable factors can impact it. Small business entrepreneurs are resilient, passionately determined and emotionally absorbed in what they do – I hope you agree after reading these inspiring stories.

Small Business Enterprises: Theory and Contributions

Small business enterprises have a positive impact on society in many different ways, including creating employment, generating income in the local community, contributing to local identity and bringing visitors to the area. They also have a wider positive social impact on society.

Early conceptualisation of responsible business and consumer behaviours focused on the environmental dimensions of their impact, while current strategies consider the wider social responsibilities of small businesses and managerial decision-making. Consumers have become accustomed to contemplating the environmental (nature) and the social setting (people and society) when considering who to purchase from and what to purchase (Hosta & Zabkar, 2021). The environmental and social impact of small businesses is frequently underestimated. There is an assumption that small businesses do not have the funds to invest in targeting environmentally and socially conscious consumers; however, focusing on the environment and society can be a differentiation factor, and investment in these areas can lead to profit and customer loyalty. As Kiranantawat and Ahmad (2022) state, sustainability is continually steering customer choices and increasingly becoming a priority for small businesses as it requires creativity and innovation.

Sustainability

Sustainability is an approach to business strategy that meets the needs of society and people today while not compromising the lives of future generations (Wolniak, 2015).

Demonstrating concern about ecological footprints and the implementation of sustainable practices can be a source of added value for small business enterprises (Topleva & Propkopov 2019), and genuine sustainability strategies go beyond token greenwashing, in which businesses invest in green marketing communications in order to be perceived as eco-friendly and sustainably engaged (Netto et al., 2020). To achieve sustainability, companies must integrate social and environmental concerns in their business strategies, placing their responsibility for these issues above, or at least equal to, profit and brand share. They must aim to achieve the triple bottom line: positive economic, environmental and social impact for people and the planet (Elkington, 1994).

Interest in and empathy with the environment and society has amplified significantly in recent years, with businesses considering sustainability as a core element of their business strategies. Concerns about sustainability and society have led to environmentally friendly business decision-making (Alwandani & Ndubisi, 2019).

Genuinely sustainable business strategies that make a clear contribution to society include eco-friendly production processes, sustainable raw materials, environmentally

https://doi.org/10.1515/9783110756142-002

friendly packaging and transportation, a positive approach to supply-chain equity and an understanding of the consequences of ecological and social decision-making. Such approaches include, for example, the circular economy, re-use, recycling and the sustainable sourcing of materials and ingredients.

The Circular Economy

The circular economy is a systems solution framework that tackles global challenges like climate change, biodiversity loss, waste and pollution. It is based on three principles: eliminate waste and pollution, circulate products and materials (at their highest value) and regenerate nature (Haines-Gadd et al., 2022).

Deutz (2020) defines the circular economy as an economic system that aims to maximise the use of resources and minimise waste and its disposal by implementing concepts such as eco-design; life-cycle analysis, which quantifies the environmental impact of a product from raw-material sources through to production, use and disposal; and closing the loop of a product's life-cycle by recirculating materials in the economy rather than creating waste by disposing of them.

> The first principle of the circular economy is to eliminate waste and pollution. Currently, our economy works in a take–make–waste system. We take raw materials from the Earth; we make products from them and eventually we throw them away as waste. Much of this waste ends up in landfills or incinerators and is lost. This system cannot work in the long term because the resources on our planet are finite. Ellen MacArthur (2023)

In a perfect circular-economy world, products are designed considering how materials can re-enter the economy at the end of their first life, turning the established, mainstream, linear approach of *make, use* and *dispose* into a circular approach of *make, use* and *re-use*. As businesses strive to achieve this, they tend to focus on the refurbishment and remanufacture of products and materials.

The concept of the circular economy has gained the interest of policymakers, influencing governments and intergovernmental agencies at local, regional, national and international levels (Geissdoerfer et al., 2017). Consumer awareness and interest in circular-economy products are evolving across many sectors with customers willing to invest time in researching the circular-economy credentials of a brand and willing to pay a higher price for sustainability they trust. Petro (2022) found that consumers across all generations are willing to pay more for sustainable products, with 90% of Generation X[1] consumers willing to pay 10% more.

Testa et al. (2020) found that, in order to persuade customers to make circular-economy purchase choices, companies must communicate clear, unambiguous infor-

---

1 Consumers born between 1965 and 1980.

mation about the circular-economy characteristics of a product in a format that can be easily shared and understood. In order to achieve this in the mainstream market, businesses must invest in educating consumers and persuading them to alter their buying behaviours to adopt sustainable products and services – consumer behaviour is key to the success of the circular economy (Joshi, 2022). Research by the Exeter Centre for Circular Economy and Business, Exeter University (2022) stresses the role of consumers and the need for organisations to engage them through participation in re-use and repurposing, returning packaging, repair schemes and second-life products – customer behaviour is central to creating a less wasteful, resource-intense world.

> In a circular economy, there is an expectation and hope that customers will become stewards of products. As a result, customer journeys will evolve into continuous loops of engagement and interaction with organizations, all so we can ensure products and materials retain their value and are kept within the system. Merryn Haines-Gadd (2022)

A circular economy not only achieves sustainability objectives but also offers an opportunity for economic growth – waste has a monetary value. The circularity potential of secondary production has a monetary value through the creation of new products from waste, which avoids the economic drain of a linear economy in which waste is collected and disposed of at both financial and environmental costs (Savini, 2023).

Small business owners have the power to implement sustainability at all levels of decision-making because they have control over every aspect of their business. They have the power to contribute to the elimination of waste, for example, by introducing the use of 100% recycled materials in clothing products or giving a second life to office-workspace waste such as furniture and flooring.

Small Business Enterprises: A Social Conscious and Societal Benefits

There is a commonly held belief that organisations must seek to balance a profit orientation, growth and economic development, and enhancement of the positive impact of consumerism on communities and society (Marchini et al., 2020).

As Marchini et al. (2023) state in later work, there are evolving, modern business enterprises that aim to integrate sustainability, ethics and societal benefits alongside economic growth, moving towards the application of business models in which the concept of ethics and sustainability is core to decisions around product design, production and operational management. These new business models combine the attributes of profit and non-profit business orientations, contributing positively to society while generating economic revenue. Doing good is good for business (Boston Consulting Group, 2023).

Small business enterprises are at the heart of local communities and are increasingly adopting the philosophy of 'profit with a purpose' by establishing a balance between pro-social behaviour and profitability (Besley & Ghatak, 2017). Socially conscious consumers demand that businesses make a societal commitment. Increasingly, consumers, particularly Generation Z[2] consumers, will only buy products from businesses that demonstrate environmental and social responsibility, and they question the social impact of brands in society (Miranda Group, 2023). Gartenberg and Serafeim (2019) found that businesses with a purpose and that have a positive impact on society outperform the market by 5% to 7% per year.

> Businesses with a purpose have a better chance of success in the modern world. Apart from being financially viable, such businesses can also be socially relevant for a long time. Therefore, purpose and profit are not mutually exclusive coordinates. They are symbiotic to the point where one cannot exist without the other. Miranda Group (2023)

One business model for achieving sustainable and social goals is social enterprise. Social Enterprise UK (2023) defines a social enterprise as a business that seeks to make a profit and succeed commercially. However, how they operate, who they employ, and how they use their profits transform lives and communities across the UK and around the world.

Social Enterprise UK (2023) stipulates that, to gain the status and accreditation of a social enterprise, a business must:
– have a clear social or environmental mission stated in governing documents
– be controlled independently and earn more than half its income through trading
– re-invest or donate at least half of all profits to its mission
– be transparent in the way it operates and supports its mission.

The difference between a social enterprise and a business with a positive social impact is that the former has its cause or mission at the core of its purpose, while the latter may have multiple core purposes – profit with a purpose rather than purpose with a profit. Some small businesses have chosen to formalise their positive social impact by registering with B Lab as B Corporation.[3]

Gaining B Corp Certification requires a business to meet sustainable, environmental and people standards, demonstrating accountability and transparency including employee benefits, charitable donations, ethical supply chains and engagement in the community and employee benefits (B Lab, 2023).

Small business enterprises often address social needs in the community such as homelessness, mental health, modern slavery and the needs of marginal members of

---

2 Consumers born between 1990 and 2000.

3 'B Lab is the non-profit network transforming the global economy to benefit all people, communities and the planet. We won't stop until all business is a force for good.' www.bcorporation.net

society, people with disabilities and the long-term unemployed. During the height of the COVID-19 pandemic, they provided local community support, including for the National Health Service and local care homes. Small business social enterprise is effectively a business model that addresses social needs and pursues social change (Luke & Chu, 2013). This is achieved through education and knowledge creation and empowerment through employment.

Education and Knowledge Creation

The activities of small business enterprises may intentionally, or inadvertently, lead to education and knowledge creation through their strategic approach to sustainability and social enterprise, and communication about their activities.

Targeted consumers and the wider public can be informed about social issues through the marketing strategies of a small business brand that educates people about issues that are new to them. Small business enterprises often create awareness through their promotional activities (e.g. events and product-labelling information) and through social media campaigns that share information about social issues such as homelessness and modern slavery, as well as their efforts to tackle such problems.

Ceira (2023) succinctly demonstrates how social media can be harnessed to educate and create awareness of social good. Strategies recommended by the team at Georgetown University Center for Social Impact Communication (2023) include sharing facts and stories and celebrating the voice of the consumer:

- *Sharing facts* via thought-provoking online stories created by independent and credible sources. People like to learn new things and small businesses can enlighten their target audience not only about products but also about the social benefits their products provide and *why*. In sharing facts, the *why* element of communication is the key to educating people about a cause in the community that they would otherwise not be aware of. Creative images engage a target audience and generate knowledge about a cause, for example, facts about male mental health issues, the number of homeless people in a community and, during the COVID-19 pandemic, the lack of hand sanitiser in hospitals and social care facilities.
- *Sharing stories* about the social benefits provided by a small business enterprise to the community garners interest and attention. Photographs of events and pictures of people who have helped others create a narrative can lead to knowledge development. It is important that small businesses let the community know how they are making a difference by creating trusted messages that are genuine and heartfelt and not simply feel-good public-relations stories. Sharing stories should not be mistaken for boastful, self-interested marketing. Storytelling is one of the best ways to develop public interest and involvement in a social cause.
- *Celebrating the voice of the consumer.* The consumer voice often has more resonance than that of a brand and celebrating this can help educate a community,

for example, through the voices of disadvantaged employees who have benefited from training and nurturing in a small business setting; a health-service provider in need of hand sanitiser during the COVID-19 pandemic; the happy outcome of a town brought together by a flood or lockdown. Both traditional (television, radio and newspapers) and social media are keen to share good outcomes and positive actions in the community. Small businesses need to cultivate consumer opinion to extend the educational reach of their causes.

There is evidence (Thorpe 2017) that small business enterprises have created awareness of poverty, homelessness, modern slavery, mental health, social exclusion and inclusion, and how civic collaboration (e.g. between towns and sports clubs) can positively contribute to the spirit of the local community.

Sharing stories helps build a relationship with customers who are interested in both the product and the social benefit of the brand. Customers learn from these stories and often become interested in the issue being shared, including the extent of modern slavery in society (Cherry, 2023), the sustainable impact of becoming a plant-based organisation (Torkington, 2022) and discovering the extensive role of seaweed in climate-change mitigation (Ross et al., 2023).

Empowerment Through Employment

Research suggests that small business enterprises can empower disadvantaged employees and the unemployed (Rotar et al., 2019) and support those who face challenges of exclusion (including physical and mental health disabilities; self-doubt, anxiety and lack of confidence; substance addiction; and health diagnoses such as autism) to gain employment.

People who are marginalised in society face social and economic obstacles to training and employment. They experience lower rates of employment and limited employment choices; where employment is available, it is often unskilled with no training or developmental prospects (Meltzer et al., 2018). The work of Meltzer et al. (2018) focuses on the contribution of social enterprises in providing meaningful employment to marginalised members of a community. They cite the work of Durie and Wilson (2017), Forrester-Jones et al. (2010) and Social Traders (2009) who identify the benefits of employment in social enterprises for marginalised employees. These benefits include a sense of independence and belonging, training and skill development leading to long-term employment, increased self-esteem and assimilation into the wider community.

Small social enterprises and small businesses with a strong social mission that employ marginalised members of society have an opportunity to ensure employee well-being while providing workplace skill development and training. It is imperative that well-being interventions are integrated into the daily activities of marginalised employees, with programmes of care tailored to individual employee needs. As asserted by Cook and Willetts (2019), organisations that employ homeless people (and those who belong to other disadvantaged groups) should provide a working environment and culture that improves self-esteem, supports emotional, social and mental health and well-being and ensures long-term employment through a strategic approach to the needs of individuals in the workplace environment. Such support can change lives.

Small Family Business Enterprises

There are 4.8 million family businesses in the UK, employing 13 million people and contributing £575 billion to the UK economy (Oxford Economics, 2020).

> Achieving sustainable, equitable prosperity is crucial to developing the UK as a fair and equal society. KPMG (2017) highlight that family businesses offer an alternative form of capitalism based on trust, reputation and long-termism. Glover and Trehan (2020, p. 4).

Family businesses positively contribute not only to the economy but also to communities and society.

Ward and Brian (2022) recognise that family businesses engage with the local community by getting involved with charities and local social causes, providing environmental and sustainable enhancement, supporting local training and long-term employment, supporting local suppliers, enriching the wider community and often having a long-term commitment to a town or city.

Family-owned enterprises tend to have strong moral governance and a long-term commitment to their business, while also demonstrating innovation and resilience (Kamenetzky, 2022). Kamenetzky (2022) found that family-owned businesses demonstrate a strong ethical philosophy in business decision-making that shapes the organisation's culture.

Family-owned businesses have ties to the local community as they are embedded in the area, particularly in the case of small towns. Neihm et al. (2008) found that social, ethical and responsible business decisions lead to the long-term sustainability of family businesses in rural communities.

The influence of the character and behaviour of family-member employees on the business was investigated by Reck et al. (2022), who found that three aspects of a family business owner's leadership and managerial style influence how they perceive ethical and social decision-making:
1. Their ability to have freedom in decision-making.
2. The blending of personal and business lives.
3. Collective employee and family business owner's values of trust, transparency and loyalty.

Family Business Enterprises: Planning for the Future

A daunting, often overlooked, aspect of a family business is succession or the exit strategy (Bernard, 2022), which is one of the most overwhelming decisions faced by a family business owner (Liebowitz, 2011). Planning for the future is an important topic of discussion in a family business, and succession can be stressful and challenging. Traditionally, the preference was for family members who are actively involved in the business to take on full responsibility and ownership over time. However, modern family business owners are increasingly choosing options other than family succession or inheritance. They understand the challenges of succession and are embracing new and evolving opportunities to plan for the future (Kamath, 2022).

Not everyone chooses to keep the business in the family, and there are many reasons why an owner of a family business may choose to sell it on, including retirement, changing career paths or there being no one in the family with the expertise or desire to continue the business. If succession is not a viable option, families often look for buyout opportunities; private-equity firms are increasingly targeting smaller businesses to take over/buy out, including long-term, family-owned organisations, which ensures a future for the company and a profitable outcome for the family (Gottfried, 2022).

An increasingly popular alternative to a buyout is employee ownership, a mechanism that transfers ownership of a family business to its employees, overseen by a board of trustees. Employee Ownership Trusts[4] have developed significantly over the last few years, a trend that protects the business legacy, retains employees' jobs and enables family business owners to move on to new pastures (Employee Ownership Wales, 2023).

> It [employee ownership] means a significant and meaningful stake in a business for all employees. It creates successful businesses in which employees enjoy working and which deliver wider benefits. The longevity of companies with employee ownership is impressive. Employee ownership is an adaptable concept and, whatever the business or the stage a business has reached, employee ownership can work well. The Nuttall Review of Employee Ownership, Nuttall (2012)

Small Business Enterprises – The Possibilities

Small business enterprises not only provide products and services but also educate communities about societal issues, often presenting solutions to combat societal problems through community members involvement, and partnerships with charities and local organisations.

---

4 https://businesswales.gov.wales/socialbusinesswales/employee-ownership

Small business enterprises inform consumers and communities about the possibilities of change, the possibilities of action and the possibilities of making positive connections between businesses, people and society.

References

Alwandani, R., & Ndubisi, N. (2019). Sustainable family business: The role of stakeholder involvement, mindful organizing, and contingent human factors. *Sustainable Family Business*, *41*(7), 945–965.

B Lab. (2023). https://www.bcorporation.net/en-us/certification

Benefit Corporation Movement. (2023). https://www.bcorporation.net/en-us/

Bernard, L. (2022). *The family business*. Business Expert Press.

Besley, T., & Ghatak, M. (2017). Profit with purpose? A theory of social enterprise. *American Economic Journal: Economic Policy*, *9*(3), 19–58.

Boston Consulting Group. (2023). Climate change and sustainability. https://www.bcg.com/capabilities/climate-change-sustainability/overview.

Ceira, R. (2023). 9 Ways to Use Social Media for Social Good. *Centre for Social Impact Communications*. https://csic.georgetown.edu/magazine/9-ways-use-social-media-social-good/.

Cherry, J. (2023). Modern slavery and the UK. UK Parliament report. https://www.parliament.uk/business/commons/committee-corridor-podcast/committee-corridor-modern-slavery-and-the-uk/

Cook, M., & Willetts, M. (2019). Affiliations for homeless individuals through social enterprise employment. *Social Enterprise Journal*, *15*(2), 215–232.

Deutz, P. (2020). Circular economy. In *International encyclopedia of human geography* (pp. 193–201). ScienceDirect.

Durie, S., & Wilson, L. (2017). *Six Mary's Place: Social return on investment report*. Series Report No. 1, Forth Sector, Edinburgh.

Elkington, J. (1994). Towards the sustainable corporation: Win-win-win business strategies for sustainable development. *California Management Review*, *36*(2), 90–100.

Employee Ownership Wales. (2023). https://employeeownershipwales.co.uk

Exeter Centre for Circular Economy, University of Exeter. (2022). New customer behaviours are key to developing circular economy, report finds. *Phys.Org*. https://phys.org/news/2022-07-customer-behaviours-key-circular-economy.html

Forrester-Jones, R., Gore, N., & Melling, K. (2010). How many people with intellectual disability are employed in the UK. *Tizard Learning Review*, *15*, 56–58.

Gartenberg, C., & Serafeim, G. (2019). 181 Top CEOs have realized companies need a purpose beyond profit. *Harvard Business Review*, 20 August.

Geissdoerfer, M., Savaget, P., Bocken, N., & Hultink, E. (2017). The circular economy – A new sustainability paradigm? *Journal of Cleaner Production*, *143*, 757–768.

Glover, J., & Trehan, K. (2020). What is the socio-economic contribution of family firms in the UK? A review of the evidence. *State of the Art Review*, *45*.

Gottfried, M. (2022). Who will inherit the family business? Often, it's private equity: Better known after billion-dollar buyouts, private equity firms are bending over backward to court family business. *Wall Street Journal*.

Haines-Gadd, M. M. S., MaGuire, S., Salter, N., & Fouest, L. (2022). Engaging consumers in a circular economy. *The Exeter Centre for Circular Economy and Clarasys Report*. https://www.clarasys.com/wp-content/uploads/2022/11/Engaging-Customers-in-a-Circular-Economy.pdf

Hosta, M., & Zabkar, V. (2021). Antecedents of environmentally and socially responsible consumer behaviour. *Journal of Business Ethics*, *171*, 273–293.

Joshi, A. (2022). Consumer behaviour is key to developing a circular economy. *Circular Innovation Lab*. https://www.circularinnovationlab.com/post/consumer-behaviour-is-key-to-developing-a-circular-economy

Kamath, K. (2022). The start-up families: How old family businesses are changing with times. *Business Today*.

Kamenetzky, D. (2022). How family businesses service hard times. *The Financial Times*, 30th June.

KPMG. (2017). Family businesses – a model for 'new' capitalism? Online post by Ken McCracken, Head of Family Business Consulting at KPMG. https://www.ifb

Liebowitz, B. (2011). *The family business: The dynamics of the family owned firm*. Business Expert Press.

Luke, B., & Chu, V. (2013). Social enterprise versus social entrepreneurship: An examination of the 'why' and 'how' in pursuing social change. *International Small Business Journal, 31*(7), 764–784.

MacArthur, E. (2023). Eliminate waste and pollution. https://www.ellenmacarthurfoundation.org/eliminate-waste-and-pollution.

Marchini, P. L., Mazza, T., & Medioli, A. (2020). Corruption and sustainable development: The impact on income shifting in European international groups. *Corporate Social Responsibility and Environmental Management, 27*, 717–730.

Marchini, P., Tibiletti, V., Fellegara, A., & Mazza, T. (2023). Pursuing a strategy of 'common benefit' in business: The adoption of the benefit corporation model in Italy. *Business Strategy and the Environment, 32*, 1481–1503.

Meltzer, A., Kayess, R., & Bates, S. (2018). Perspectives of people with intellectual disability about open, sheltered, and social enterprise employment. *Social Enterprise Journal, 14*(2), 255–244.

Miranda Group. (2023). Businesses gain when purpose and profit go hand in hand. *Forbes*, 20 January.

Netto, S., Sobral, M., Ribeiro, A., & Soares, G. (2020). Concepts and forms of greenwashing: A systematic review. *Environmental Sciences Europe, 32*(19).

Neihm, L., Swinney, J., & Miller, N. (2008). Community social responsibility and its consequences for family business performance. *Journal of Small Business Management, 46*(3), 331–350.

Nuttall, G. (2012). The Nuttall review of employee ownership. https://assets.publishing.service.gov.uk/media/sharing-success-nuttall-review-employee-ownership.pdf

Oxford Economics. (2020). *The State of the Nation: The UK family business sector 2020–21*. Oxford Economics.

Petro, G. (2022). Consumers demand sustainable products and shopping formats. *Forbes*, 11 March.

Reck, F., Fischer, D., & Brettel, M. (2022). Ethical decision-making in family firms: The role of employee identification. *Journal of Business Ethics, 180*, 651–673.

Ross, F., Boydd, P., Filbee-Dexter, K., Watanabe, K., Ortega, A., Krause-Jensen, D., Lovelock, C., Sondak, C., Bach, L., Duarte, C., Serrano, O., Beardall, J., Tarbuck, P., & Macreadi, P. (2023). Potential role of seaweeds in climate change mitigation. *Science of the Total Environment, 885*.

Rotar, L., Pamić, R., & Bojnec, S. (2019). Contributions of small and medium enterprises to employment in the European Union countries. *Economic Research-Ekonomska Istraživanja, 32*(1), 3302–3314.

Savini, F. (2023). Futures of the social metabolism: Degrowth, circular economy and the value of waste. *Futures, 50*, 103–180.

Social Enterprise UK. (2023). All about social enterprises. https://www.socialenterprise.org.uk/all-about-social-enterprise/

Social Traders. (2009). Social firms: social enterprise – into brief. Social Traders Ltd, Victoria.

Testa, F., Iovino, R., & Iraldo, F. (2020). The circular economy and consumer behaviour: The mediating role of information seeking in buying circular packaging. *Business Strategy and the Environment, 29*(8), 3435–3448.

Thorpe, D. (2017, 12 September). The role of entrepreneurship in ending poverty and homelessness. *Forbes*.

Topleva, S., & Prokopov, T. (2019). Integrated business model for sustainability of small and medium-sized enterprises in the food industry. *British Food Journal, 122*(5).

Torkington, S. (2022, October). Vegan, vegetarian or flexitarian? Three ways to eat more sustainably. *World Economic Forum*.

Ward, M., & Brian, P. (2022). The contribution of family businesses to local communities in the UK. *Research Briefing, House of Commons Library*.

Wolniak, R. (2015). Reporting process of corporate social responsibility and greenwashing. In: 15th International Multidisciplinary Scientific Geoconference SGEM2015, Ecology, Economics, Education, and Legislation. https://doi.org/10.5593/sgem2015/b53/s21.06353

Part One: **Social Impact: A Positive Impact on Society**

Manumit Coffee Roasters (Source: Dai Hankey).

Rifhat Qureshi Modest Trends London (Source: Rifhat Qureshi).

https://doi.org/10.1515/9783110756142-003

This part discusses six small business enterprise case studies that have a positive social impact on society which have been created through their strategic approach to sustainability and engagement with their community:

Rype Office is a small business that creates sustainable, greener and low-cost beautiful office spaces.

Zajac Ranch for Children is an accessible summer camp for Canadian children of all abilities.

Skipper Otto is a community-based fishery that supports Canadian fishing families by trading on sustainable seafood policies and practices.

Manumit Coffee Roasters trains and employs survivors of modern-day slavery who are rebuilding their lives.

The Goodwash Company produces sustainable luxury skin care for humans and pets.

Modest Trends London is a fashion brand producing sustainable and ethical abaya, hijabs and modest fashion.

Rype Office

This chapter is based on a case study developed from ideas and research generated by Lisa Griffith during her undergraduate studies at Cardiff Business School.

Synopsis

Dr Greg Lavery is the founder of the office furniture re-manufacturer Rype Office. He started with a background in civil engineering and went on to discover his passion for sustainability later on, when he completed his PhD in green buildings at a time before sustainability and green business was being seriously considered. He gained his PhD and developed his business background while working for and growing some of the world's biggest companies to market leadership, continuously keeping profitable sustainability at the centre of his purpose. Greg combined his passion for design and building founding Rype Office in 2014, a company that cares about climate change and waste and which has now become one of the top office furniture re-manufacturer in the UK. With no other big players to compete with, it was the first of its kind – employing a whole new business approach that largely disrupted the traditional value chain economy.

https://doi.org/10.1515/9783110756142-004

Dr. Greg Lavery (Source: Greg Lavery).

Themes

The traditional value chain economy heavily features waste and environmental damage, with 300 tonnes of office furniture going to recycling or landfill every day in the UK. The circular economy flips the process and starts with the customer, ensuring that they understand what it is that they want and don't want, what they already have that can be worked with, and ultimately giving them a tailor-made, *beautiful* outcome (Lavery, 2021). Rype provides free design services and the innovative service of auditing of existing furniture, re-using items where possible. Rype sources used furniture and re-manufacture it into new sustainable products at a fraction of the traditional market price, without compromising quality (customers can't tell the difference). Rype also has its own lines of new furniture made from recycled materials that re-use waste plastic, giving the products longer life as they can be re-manufactured over and over again and shouldn't need to end up in landfill. The aim here is to get a purpose-value-led discussion going. Additionally, unlike any of the other traditional office furniture giants, Rype guarantees take back of used furniture that is no longer needed, saving huge costs in sourcing of products and materials, and ultimately making a profit while reducing waste. Their main argument for why other companies have failed to capitalise on this opportunity is due to rigid set of traditional value chains and inability to change traditional supplier policies.

Rype circular economy furniture (Source: Greg Lavery).

When Greg first set up Rype Office, his aim for the company was to push sustainability as hard as possible through the *triple bottom line* of economic, environmental and social benefit.

Rype Office has some of the best UK architects and designers working on their projects and products; their circular economy approach has provided over 7,000 hours of Real Living Wage work and training for local long-term unemployed people with disabilities, giving them a step up onto the employment ladder once their projects with Rype had ended, if they chose to do so elsewhere.

Suppliers and partners that have worked with Rype all share values around sustainability and social benefit, including social enterprises like the Merthyr Tydfil Institute for the Blind and Greenstream Flooring. The result is that their marketing, to a certain degree, takes care of itself as working with passionate people, who voluntarily seek projects for Rype (including Cardiff Business School) to help them succeed.

Small Business Enterprise

Greg demonstrates creative destruction as an entrepreneur, simply put, he is leading in re-organising an industry. Forms of entrepreneurial motivation, i.e. the reasons why entrepreneurs do what they do, include the desire to build something from the ground up, the determination to compete and succeed, and the happiness and satisfaction that result from successfully resolving a social, economic or environmental problem through creative problem-solving. On the flip side, factors that create obstacles and therefore inhibit entrepreneurial action will automatically be more difficult to conceptualise, plan and fully understand than something that has already been established and accepted for a longer period of time. Our natural tendency as humans to resist deviating from routines acts as a mental blocker, even if what is being worked on is a better alternative. Even worse is the pressure to perform successfully to avoid the social disapproval that tends to come hand in hand with making mistakes or perceived failures. It is widely agreed that the role of an entrepreneur is central to change because they *disturb the economic status quo through innovations* (Goss, 2005). However, something that we cannot ignore is the problem of embedded agency; by elevating these motivational features, other aspects fall into the background, including the explanation behind how entrepreneurs use resources and relations available to overcome these obstacles (Holm, 1995). Rype Office is an excellent example of how creativity, innovation and meaningful entrepreneurship hold a significant amount of power when it comes to changing how organisations design, source and supply office furniture.

NHS Public Health Wales (Source: Greg Lavery).

The Future

Rype has embraced the opportunity to introduce a new business model and a new structural market approach that seeks to transform the traditional office furniture marketplace through sustainable innovation. Greg is the leader in sustainable office re-manufacture. Revolutionising change in sectors of the business economy long steeped in traditional business practices.

References

Goss, D. (2005). Schumpeter's legacy? Interaction and emotions in the sociology of entrepreneurship. *Entrepreneurship Theory and Practice, 29,* 205–218.

Holm, P. (1995). The dynamics of institutionalization: Transformation processes in Norwegian fisheries. *Administrative Science Quarterly, 40,* 398–422.

Lavery, G. (2021). *Speaker programme.* Presentation of Rype Office.

Rype Office. (2022). Rype Office. https://rypeoffice.com/

Zajac Ranch for Children: Strategy in the Non-Profit Sector

Carolyn Strong, Adam Mills and Tia Dalupang

> Anna gave camp 11 out of 10 this year. Her favorite year so far. It is the first time this year she has felt she was with 'friends.' She felt like she fit in and was very happy. Thank you for creating a very unique place for my daughter to feel good about herself. Parent of Anna, age 15 (Spina Bifida/Turner Syndrome Camp)

Synopsis

Carmen Zajac was making one of her regular visits to the Zajac Ranch on a sunny Wednesday during one of the camp weeks in July. While overlooking the lake, watching the kids having fun swimming and jumping off the dock, she thought back to when the ranch opened its doors for the first time in 2004. The summer camps and facilities had come a long way since then. She was proud of what she and her family had accomplished in providing youth with illnesses and disabilities the opportunity to experience the joys of summer camp. The Zajac Foundation was grateful to have a devout group of donors that they were able to maintain a relationship with over the years. But she knew that there was a lot of work to be done. As donors were aging and economic times were getting tougher, she knew that the Zajac team was going to have to work hard and be creative if they wanted to keep the ranch alive and well for many years to come. On one hand, she needed to find new ways to connect with a new generation of donors. On the other hand, her ultimate goal was to find a way to make the ranch a completely self-sustainable non-profit enterprise.

History

Mel Zajac was passionate about giving back to the community in which he lived. Throughout his life, he helped many children through various fundraising efforts whenever he could. He realised, however, that both children and senior citizens were among the most vulnerable groups in society, and that he could make a difference in British Columbia (BC) by reaching out to others to raise both awareness and funds. Involving his wife, Irene and daughters Carmen, Corinne and Karen, over the past four decades, Mel and his family had raised and contributed over $18 million to those in need of support throughout the Lower Mainland of BC.

Mel and Irene founded the Zajac Classic Golf Tournament, which had become, over the past 47 years, not only the longest-running but also one of the most celebrated and successful charity golf tournaments in BC. The tournament was used to

https://doi.org/10.1515/9783110756142-005

raise funds for causes such as the BC Children's Hospital and the Variety Club. Today, the tournament raises approximately $150,000 per year. In 1996, the annual Zajac Women's Golf Tournament was founded.

In 1986, a shocking tragedy struck the Zajac family. Sons Mel Jr. and Marty lost their lives in separate sporting accidents only 8 months apart. Never fully recovering from the unexpected and overwhelming loss but recognising the need to go on, Mel Zajac wanted to do something to keep the memory of his sons alive, who themselves had also worked with disadvantaged youth during their short lives. Wanting to create a legacy that would continue to give back to the community for years to come, Mel and Irene established a charitable organisation, The Mel Jr. and Marty Zajac Foundation, with a personal contribution of $100,000. They continued to raise funds and eventually established an endowment at the United Way in memory of Mel Jr. and Marty. The mandate of The Zajac Foundation, as it has come to be known, was to 'support children, seniors and those with special needs through innovative community projects focused on developing lifelong skills and independence.' The Foundation focused – and continues to focus – on building relationships and building communities by strengthening the social ties that support and nourish people, thereby improving quality of life.

Since its inception, the Foundation has made a significant impact in the community through various projects, including:
- The Zajac Norgate House, in North Vancouver, for seniors and people with disabilities.
- The Sandcastle Developmental Preschool in Mission, providing integrative programs for children with special needs.
- Capital support for the BC Centre for Ability, a non-profit society that promotes successful community participation for individuals with disabilities.
- The Zajac Summer Swim Camp for athletes of all abilities.
- Marketing innovation
  - Products
  - Promotional innovation
- Relationship with communities
  - Customers
  - Challenges
- The future

Small Business Enterprise

Non-Profit Organisations and Registered Charities

For-profit and non-profit organisations function in many similar ways. Importantly, like for-profit businesses, non-profit organisations (NPOs) have the ability to generate financial revenues. However, if the NPO does choose to generate revenue, these are strictly used to benefit the organisation and its projects, rather than to benefit share-holders as with for-profit firms.

NPOs are organised at the provincial level, and can be granted non-profit status in as little as two weeks from the Government of BC. These NPOs can operate for pur-poses of social welfare, civic improvement, pleasure, recreation or any other purpose except financial profit. Because NPOs are dedicated to benefiting the public, they do not pay corporate income tax.

Within the NPO classification, an organisation can further apply to become a regis-tered charity. All official charities must be registered in Canada through a thorough and lengthy federal designation process with the Canada Revenue Agency. Designation as a charitable organisation means that the NPO can operate solely for charitable pur-poses, such as poverty relief, advancement of education or religion, or purposes benefi-cial to the community. Only a registered charity, importantly, has the ability to issue government-recognised income tax receipts to individual donors. The Zajac Foundation is both an NPO and a fully registered charity with the Canadian government.

The Zajac Ranch for Children

In a study conducted by the Canadian Council of Social Development (2021), almost 90% of responding Canadian service-providing agencies reported that the needs of children and youth with special needs were being unmet in their communities, and identified recreational services as one of these unmet needs. The Council concluded that 'public services do not sufficiently recognise the extra demands placed on the families of children with disabilities, and the families need better financial, physical, social and emotional supports.' Canadian Council of Social Development (2021).

Recognising the gap in recreation facilities capable of serving children with a va-riety of medical conditions (most facilities offered specialised care for specific condi-tions), Mel and the Zajac Foundation team embarked on its most ambitious project, with the creation of the Zajac Ranch for Children in 2004. The Zajac Ranch was an accessible western-style ranch and camp with an onsite medical centre, designed to welcome all children with serious and chronic illnesses and disabilities. The organisa-tion met a specific need for innovative community services that support children with disabilities and serious and chronic illnesses in BC. Since 2004, the Zajac Ranch had welcomed thousands of children ages 7–17 with a variety of medical conditions, in-cluded (but not limited to) autism spectrum disorder, blood disorders, craniofacial dif-ferences, Down syndrome, muscular dystrophy multiple organ transplants, spina bifida, Tourette syndrome, Turner syndrome and more.

Set amidst Crown forestlands on the shores of Stave Lake in Mission, BC, the Zajac Ranch for Children was a forty-acre west coast oasis that welcomed children with serious and chronic illnesses and disabilities. Their mission was to raise the spi-

rits and transform the lives of special children by providing the joy and magic of summer camp and a therapeutic outdoor recreation experience that all children should have the opportunity to experience. The Zajac Ranch embraced seven core values:
- **RESPECT** and appreciation for the value and diversity we each represent
- **INCLUSIVE** opportunities that welcome all participants regardless of ability
- **EMPOWER** through opportunities
- **COMPASSION** empathy and concern for the well-being of others
- **INTEGRITY** and consideration for one another
- **EMBRACE** the possibilities
- **EXPERIENCE** the thrill of participating

Mel Zajac, at the beginning, had no idea how to run summer camps, but he was a hard-working innovator with a vision. In order to accomplish their mission, Mel Zajac's ultimate goal was for the ranch to be self-sustainable with fully equipped facilities to cater to all medical needs.

The fully wheelchair-accessible facilities at the Zajac Ranch for Children included:
- An 11,500 square foot indoor/outdoor therapeutic pool and spa complex, including a physiotherapy room and wellness exercise facility.
- An outdoor amphitheatre and fire pit with seating for up to 120, often used for guest speakers, ceremonies and performances.
- A dining lodge complete with commercial kitchen, to prepare and serve meals for up to 120 guests at a time.
- A large recreation hall for meetings and activities.
- A covered outdoor picnic area with a large barbeque, ideal for meals, receptions or informal outdoor meetings regardless of the weather.
- An indoor horseback-riding arena.

The Zajac Ranch for Children is equipped to allow youth of all disabilities to participate in all programming. In addition to the accessible facilities, they are also able to offer the following activities to all guests: hiking the wheelchair-accessible nature trails, swimming, kayaking, canoeing, fishing, indoor and outdoor horseback riding, archery, high and low ropes courses, a climbing wall, team building activities and therapeutic horseback riding. The ranch provided facilities not only for physical exercise but also a venue for wellness of the mind (Table 1).

There was no other camp of its kind in the BC, and the Zajac Ranch was the only camp to accept and support campers from across the country, sponsoring travel costs for out-of-town children. The ranch also had the only 24-hour onsite medical centre with facilities and medical staff to care for children with different medical conditions at the same time. The medical centre was staffed by volunteer doctors and nurses, who provided round-the-clock supervision and care. In 2011 they had 36 volunteer nurses and 7 volunteer doctors. The ranch also offered higher-than-average counsel-

Table 1: Activities schedule.

Activities
( ) indicates the minimum number of staff required to run activity

Core Activities

High Ropes Alpine Challenge Course (2)	Canoeing (1/10 participants)
Low Ropes Team Development Course (1)	Kayaking (1/10 participants)
Climbing Wall (2)	Wilderness Survival (2)
Horseback Programming Activities (2)	Archery (1)

Outdoor Education Activities

Lakeshore Safari (1)	Junior Astronauts (1)
Forest Rangers (1)	Map Masters (1)
BC Bird Study (1)	Nature Art (1)
Gold Panning (1)	Orienteering (1)
Wilderness Survival (1)	Animal Adaptation (1)

Team Building Activities

Group Challenge Part 1 (1)	Cooperative Games (1)
Group Challenge Part 2 (1)	

Other/Evening Programs

Action Auction (1)	Night Explorers (1)
Camp Scavenger Hunt (1)	Liars Club (1)

lor care with a ratio of 1:1 to 1:3 counsellor-to-camper support, along with specialised programming customised to meet the needs of each medical condition.

Ranch Operations

The weeklong summer medical camps for children took place during July and August of every year. Hosting children with disabilities and chronic illnesses, their families, over 80 volunteers and 22 full-time seasonal staff did, however, come at a cost to the ranch in partnership with various organisations, Zajac Ranch had the opportunity every year to subsidise campers' camp fees; in 2011, approximately 80% of campers were subsidised fully through the Zajac Foundation sponsorship and related health organisations. For the other 20%, the campers were guaranteed at least 50% subsidy. The aim was to eventually subsidise the fees for the campers fully.

Approximately half of the funding for the ranch was via donations, often from large corporations who would "sponsor" one-week summer camp for all attendees. These organisations included Telus, the Boston Pizza Foundation, Mercedes-Benz, the Mr. Lube Foundation, Black Dog and White Spot Restaurants. Pharmasave, a national pharmacy chain, sponsored the summer camps by donating two months' worth of medical supplies to the Zajac Ranch.

The ranch also reached out to individual donors. They had an average of 500 individual donors per year, most of whom donated hundreds of dollars annually, and received income tax receipts in return. Zajac offered the opportunity for individuals to sponsor an individual child or a cabin group for $5000, although fewer numbers of individual donors chose these options.

Non-Camp Ranch Rentals

Donations alone could not support the annual income requirements for ranch operations, so Zajac was forced to diversify their strategy in order to generate an income stream. In the ten non-camp months, September through June, Zajac kept the facilities open and operating to offer site rentals for corporate meetings and retreats, religious retreats, elementary school nature activity field trips, yoga and sporting group events, conferences, and private functions such as weddings and family reunions.

Relationships with the Community

The majority of funds for both the Zajac Foundation and the Zajac Ranch, with the exception of the rental income from the ranch, comes from corporate and personal donations. As with for-profit firms, NPOs like Zajac are under pressure to compete for the limited financial resources available – competition among charities and NPOs in BC is very intense.

Zajac's donations can be classified into one of four categories:
1. Large individual donations, often from friends of Mel and the family.
2. Large corporate donations ranging from the strong Zajac brand and broad scope of charitable goals made it attractive to large companies who received both tax credit and public relations opportunities in exchange for their donations.
3. Smaller donations ranging from $500 to $5000, either from individual donors or small-to-medium sized, generally local, companies. Although Zajac does not have an official strategy for targeting donors in this bracket, these donations provided a smaller but constant stream of donor income.
4. Small individual donations, ranging from $1 to $100. Although these types of donations are generally few and far between, this is seen as a potentially lucrative opportunity for younger and less individually wealthy donors who still want to contribute, possibly on an ongoing basis. Zajac executives term this category 'Micro-Giving.'

Summer camp activities (Source: Carolyn Strong).

The Micro-Giving Community

Over the past few years, Zajac had been noticing dwindling donations from an aging base of individual donors. With increasingly unstable economic times, there were fewer jobs for graduates and Baby Boomers were less likely to retire due to dwindling savings, stocks and mortgages, both resulting in lower donations.

> Canada is experiencing significant demographic changes as the population ages, immigrants from around the globe make up an increasing portion of the population, citizens continue to move from rural to urban areas, and the population of Aboriginal youth grows. This could have important implications with respect to the makeup of Zajac Ranch for Children donors, volunteers, boards and staff, and the needs, expectations, and aspirations of the community it serves. (Imagine Canada, 2010)

With these concerns, Zajac was concerned about the long-term sustainability of their current fundraising strategy. The Foundation's executive team have been considering the concept of Micro-Giving for several reasons. First, it wants to expand its social capital and brand to a new and younger generation of donors. The Zajac brand was largely unknown to people under the age of 30 in BC, possibly by virtue of the age of the Foundation itself. Particularly since it served children and young adults at the ranch, Zajac saw an opportunity in the future to reach out to and connect with this new demographic group.

Second, the concept of Micro-Giving seemed to make sense for younger people: because of the financial situation of most young people (e.g. students), they could not afford to donate large sums of money at a time. Charitable giving overall is seen as largely inaccessible to a large proportion of the population. Zajac sees an opportunity in Micro-Giving to create ongoing revenue streams from repeat giving (e.g. $1 per week or $5 per paycheck), which, if scaled, could provide a significant and more sustainable flow of income. However, this would require a significantly large base of young donors, which would in turn require a much more concerted marketing effort.

The Future

Watching the smiles on the faces of the campers as they played in the lake, Carmen knew that she had to find a way to keep the ranch open long into the future. She knew that in order to achieve self-sustainability for the future, her team at the Zajac Foundation was going to have to address, foremost, two pressing strategic growth problems. First, they need to figure out how to generate enough revenue income and profit from the ranch and its facilities to make the ranch fully self-sustainable, and in particular, how to generate more rental business during the traditionally vacant winter months. Second, they needed to enhance social capital by creating an effective Micro-Giving model to attract and connect with a new generation of young donors.

References

Canadian Council of Social Development. (2001). *Children and Youth With Special Needs*. http://www.ccsd.ca/ pubs/2001/specialneeds/specialneeds.pdf

Imagine Canada. (2010). *A framework for action for the nonprofit sector: The drivers of change*. http://www. imaginecanada.ca/node/258#driver0

Skipper Otto: Scaling Socially Responsible Seafood

Christine Pitt, David Kerruish, Theresa Eriksson, Andrew Flostrand and Carolyn Strong

Synopsis

Skipper Otto was just wrapping up another busy summer of providing fish directly to seafood lovers. As another season came to an end, Sonia Strobel, Chief Executive Officer of Skipper Otto, contemplated what would be in store for next season. They had enjoyed a good season, meeting the demand of their expanding niche market with sustainably harvested seafood, yet Skipper Otto was facing a dilemma. It was becoming increasingly difficult to effectively manage their supply chain and this was dramatically constraining their operational scale. Many of their fish were being caught and flash-frozen at sea, processed in local processing plants and then sold directly to their customers.[1] Although this had worked in the past, this process was becoming unsustainable. Reliable access to these limited local processing services was becoming more and more constrained due to industrial competitors who were dominating local processing facilities. As local commercial processing services became increasingly scarce, a number of smaller operators had been squeezed out of dependable access to this essential service.

Doug Kostering (Source: Skipper Otto).

---

1 https://skipperotto.com

https://doi.org/10.1515/9783110756142-006

Shaun Strobel (Source: Skipper Otto).

History

Skipper Otto is Canada's first community-supported fishery (CSF), located in Vancouver on the Canadian West Coast, and was founded in 2008 by husband and wife team Sonia and Shaun Strobel. The founding of the company was inspired by Shaun's father, Otto, a local fisherman who wanted to make his catch available to local customers at a price that was fair for consumers and sustainable for fishermen like himself. It is based on a agriculture (CSA) model. A CSF model that links fishermen to a local market. Members of a CSF would pre-pay for a season of fresh, local and sustainable seafood, which they could receive as a weekly or bi-weekly share of fish or other seafood.

The Skipper Otto model is a little different from the traditional CSA. Skipper Otto had members who pre-purchased a share of the catch before the start of the fishing season. Members could log in to the online store through their website, choose whatever seafood from the available catch whenever they like, submit their orders and choose their pick-up dates and location.

Skipper Otto would then deliver the order to one of over 30 specified pick-up locations across Canada including their home base at the False Creek Fisherman's Wharf in Vancouver. The pick-up locations would often be stores that share Skipper Otto's values of providing high-quality local products. After completing their first season, word spread quickly about the access to local and ethical. Skipper Otto expanded their business, with Shaun returning to fishing alongside his father and Sonia running onshore operations. Skipper Otto also increased their range of pick-up locations across Canada with community partners ranging from grocery stores to specialty kitchen supply stores.

Small Business Enterprise

From the onset, Skipper Otto's goal was to be truly community based, supporting local fishermen, connecting them directly to local consumers. Unlike the traditional industrial fisheries, Skipper Otto had streamlined their process and cut out unnecessary intermediaries ensuring the fish was not only locally sourced but also locally processed. This allowed them to create direct connections between local fishermen and consumers, with their supply chain consisting of themselves as intermediaries between the fishing crew and the customer, with customers picking up their seafood shares from select distribution points.

During his career, Shaun's father had witnessed the changes in the fishing industry, from independent fisherman selling sustainable fish in local markets, to the present situation where large-scale enterprises now dominated the harvesting of many fisheries, predominantly serving global markets. The commercial fisheries demanded a large, complex supply chain, with one effect being the inefficient method of processing local fish for local markets. Locally caught fish was frequently transported around the world for processing and then shipped back to markets, sometimes to the area where it was harvested. Strobel's decision to simplify their supply chain was not only to connect fishermen with local customers but also based on the positive environmental and social impact of this model. Their decision regarding the structure of the supply chain was motivated by 'the joint goal of protecting ocean resources and increasing food sovereignty by creating an alternative to the dominant model of export-oriented industrial food production.'[2]

Their simplified supply chain also allowed them to provide valuable information to their customers regarding the traceability of their fish. This type of information was important for customers who were invested in where their food came from and how it was sourced. This was in part due to the rise of conscious consumers who cared about the environmental impacts of their purchases[3] but also to the murmurs of mislabelled fish that began to surface in 2010. These murmurs were confirmed in the USA by a study conducted by the foundation, Oceana.[4] In the summer of 2018, cases of fish labelling fraud were also confirmed in Canada.[5] Skipper Otto acknowledged traceability as an important decision factor among their members, explaining: 'We've cut out huge swathes of the supply chain providing you with complete transparency around what we are catching, where and how. We educate consumers around important issues in fisheries, and are rebuilding robust local food systems and communities.'[6]

The Fishermen and the Process

The Skipper Otto team comprised of locally based fishermen and onshore operational staff. Committed to supporting small-scale fishing families, 24 fishermen across British Columbia worked for Skipper Otto with Shaun as the lead fisherman. Many of the fishermen in the Skipper Otto crew had been fishermen their entire career and belong to families who are multi-generational fishermen. Skipper Otto has been committed to paying fishermen a living wage and focusing on quality over quantity. The fishermen harvest in different areas of British Columbia depending on where they live and the time of year.

As seafood is a highly perishable product, it is important to preserve the integrity of the fish. After any fish had been caught, it was immediately flash frozen to preserve

---

2 Interview with Sonia Strobel.
3 Mapping your future growth: Five game-changing consumer trends. *BDC Report*, October 2013.
4 Oceana study reveals seafood fraud nationwide. *Oceana Report*, February 2013.
5 Sagan, A. Nearly half of all seafood improperly labelled: Study. *The Globe and Mail*, 28 August 2018. https://www.theglobeandmail.com/business/article-nearly-half-of-canadian-seafood-improperly-labelled-study/
6 Interview with Sonia Strobel.

the quality and freshness. It was then brought to shore for processing, where it was cleaned, cut (e.g. filleting and freezing of fresh fish) or manufactured for fish products (e.g. lox, smoked salmon, canning).

Skipper Otto products (Source: Skipper Otto).

The Customers

When they launched operations in 2008 in preparations for the 2009 season, Skipper Otto began with 40 members for their first season. From there the number of members steadily grew through word of mouth and in 2017 they reached over 2,400 members. Skipper Otto mostly catered to individual consumers and recently started to serve restaurants. Skipper Otto had three distinct customer segments. The first segment consisted of couples without children and with strong environmental concerns, as well as retirees who have a keen interest in food culture. This segment was the largest and fastest growing of the three. The second segment was made up of mostly young families with strong social and environmental values. This group chooses to purchase fish from Skipper Otto as a way to teach their children about sustainable food. The third segment was the 'hipster' crowd, younger adults who enjoy obtaining their fish from a more unique source than a chain grocery store. They also value the experimental aspect that comes along with ordering an entire fish and discovering how to prepare it and trying new recipes. The last two segments described are smaller in terms of revenue than the first segment.

All three segments valued local produce over the convenience of obtaining seafood from chain grocery stores. They also valued the transparency with which Skipper Otto operates and the traceability of their products. 'Our price is comparable to what you would pay for a comparable product in a retail product,'[7] Sonia said while highlighting the challenges of poor transparency and misleading labelling of other seafood products.

In addition to individual members, Skipper Otto also catered to small restaurants in Toronto and Vancouver. These fine-dining restaurants placed an emphasis on the quality of the ingredients used and the sustainability and locality from which they were sourced.

The Fish and Seafood Industry

Fish and seafood are among Canada's largest exports in terms of food products, with $6.9 billion worth of fish and seafood exported. Approximately 72,000 Canadians make their living directly from fishing and fishing-related activities and it was an important economic source. Canada's most valuable exported species include lobster, Atlantic salmon, snow (queen) crab and shrimp. Although considered to some as controversial, aquaculture (fish farming) was also the fastest growing food production activity in the world and a growing sector in Canada.

Sustainable Fisheries

The Canadian government has recognised the dual importance of maintaining a sustainable yet profitable fishing industry. Fisheries and Oceans Canada takes a precautionary approach to a sustainable and responsible management of fisheries by ensuring decision-making is informed by scientific evidence and addresses the fragility of the ecosystem. A sustainable fishery involves harvesting and farming fish stocks in a way that meets present demands while preserving the ability to meet future needs. A successful model for sustainable fisheries management encompasses planning, managing environmental impacts and monitoring results. Enforcing the rules is a costly exercise and Canada has one of the most advanced programs in the world, spending approximately $130 million annually on monitoring and enforcement across the country. Many aspects of the model for sustainable fisheries are just some of the core values at the centre of the CSF movement that Sonia and Shaun Strobel are so passionate about.

---

7 Interview with Sonia Strobel.

The Processing Plant

During Skipper Otto's early years, a limited amount of processing was either completed onshore or on the vessels at sea. In some cases, the processing step was bypassed by creating a direct-to-consumer model for a small market segment whereby fish were flash-frozen whole, bagged and labelled. These processing solutions were largely sufficient for the first 10 years of operation, however they have recently been limiting the business and opportunities for growth. A number of high-end restaurants were increasingly interested in purchasing from Skipper Otto, but many restaurants require a steady, reliable supply of pre-cut and filleted fish. Although Skipper Otto has the ability to meet initial restaurant demand in terms of supply, it can only be processed at scale in a commercial fish processing facility. However, there was little dependable access to commercial processing facilities. Sonia acknowledged 'the lack of secure processing is the biggest hurdle we have to overcome,'[8] and despite years of attempting to find a solution, Skipper Otto remained without reliable access to a suitable processing facility.

Feeling that the pressure to find a plant was peaking, Sonia and her partner Shaun saw the number of members continue to grow. They also saw another big fishing season come and go. 'This year, a brood year for sockeye salmon, is a great illustration of the processing pinch point,' says Sonia. "Processing capacity in Vancouver is maxed out. All companies are scrambling.' The retail opportunity was a concern for Sonia: 'If we had, for example, a retailer approach us to buy 10,000 to 20,000 sockeye salmon, well, we don't have the processing capacity to take that opportunity.'

One option that Sonia was actively considering was operating and controlling their own processing plant. This was an idea that had been under consideration for the last 5 years since their processing partner lost their lease. Negotiations were progressing with a local First Nation, who had their own needs for custom fish processing, on a partnership to build a 12,000-square-foot fish processing plant in Greater Vancouver. The facility would employ one full-time plant manager and one full-time plant quality manager which are necessary to meet regulatory requirements. Approximately six fish-cutting staff would be employed on an as-needed basis. The forecast was for the plant to break-even in year one by operating at 30% of its capacity – one-third of which would come from meeting Skipper Otto's existing consumer needs and one-third from the First Nations partner. The final third was anticipated to come from a combination of meeting retail and hospitality and obtaining an additional First Nations partner.

In addition to fish processing, the proposed plant would include an adjoining restaurant and retail sales location. The cutters, employed primarily in the processing facility, would also support food preparation in the adjoining retail and restaurant facilities. The plant manager would ideally have some culinary training and be able

---

8 Interview with Sonia Strobel.

to identify opportunities for value-added products, such as pre-made food products like seafood burger patties.

Approximately 75% of Canadian seafood is sold to export markets while approximately 70%–80% of the seafood available to Canadians is imported.[9] This resulted in commercial local processing plants reserved almost exclusively for the export market. A curious side effect was large amounts of local fish were being sent to China to be processed only to be sold to other foreign markets or sometimes transported back to Canada to be sold to Canadian consumers. Sonia senses that the restaurant industry has not caught up to a market of consumers who want quality produce and to know where their fish comes from. She saw a need to help the retail industry get on board with traceability, and to provide local, sustainable restaurant-ready seafood.

The Future

As Sonia reflects on another busy fishing season and continued to plan for Skipper Otto, there were multiple options at hand for how to continue to scale the business. Retaining a sustainable approach, both from a fishing and a business perspective needed to remain a key focus. She contemplated how to explore growth by further leveraging restaurant and supermarket options and how to strategically guide their growth. Much of her focus was dedicated upcoming discussions with the fishery authorities and the First Nations band. As she weighed her options, she found that she was finally ready to make some choices. This required decisions ranging from how to update the business model, secure funding, scale staff and most importantly, whether to actually proceed with the processing plant. What would be required to run the existing Skipper Otto operation and at the same time build out a new type of business, the processing facility? Should the plant be completely owned and operated by Skipper Otto or should they proceed to seek a partnership agreement, such as with the First Nations band? As she weighed her options Sonia was excited, she knew that Skipper Otto would be entering new and unfamiliar territory. *'The processing facility is the biggest decision we had faced, We were deciding on a whole new business for Skipper Otto.'*

---

9 Industry overview of fish and seafood. Agriculture and Agri-Food Canada. http://www.agr.gc.ca/eng/industry-markets-and-trade/canadian-agri-food-sector-intelligence/fish-and-seafood/industry-overview/?id=1383756439917

Manumit Coffee Roasters

Synopsis

Dai Hankey is a Church planting pastor and founder of the Christian charity, Red Community in Wales. He is a former DJ, skateboard, rapper and a spoken word poet. His life aim is to help young people on the margin of society including drug addicts and young offenders.

The Red Community charity strives to fight against human trafficking through awareness, support and compassion. Dai is the founder of Manumit Coffee Roasters, an organisation that aims to help people exploited in modern-day slavery to change their lives. It exists to offer freedom and hope through ethically sourcing coffee, offering compassionate employment to people with no hope or expectations and strategically investing profits in trafficking charities and support organisations.

A modern slave is someone who has been taken against their will into prostitution, forced labour, to live in a squalid situation with no payment, including as a domestic slave with little or no reward. Modern slavery also extends to being forced into criminal situations such as living as slaves on cannabis farms and being forced into County Lines gangs where drug dealers exploit young people.

Dai Hankey (Source: Dai Hankey).

https://doi.org/10.1515/9783110756142-007

Manumit is an old English word that means to set slaves free which is the objective of this small voluntary-run enterprise coffee business.

History

As a member of the Red Community which is all about raising awareness of modern-day slavery and human trafficking in Wales, one of the projects he started was a scheme where they trained volunteers to 'befriend' those who had experienced modern-day slavery to help them restore their lives. As a result of the success of this scheme, it was discovered that some of the people being befriended wanted to move into mainstream society and gain meaningful employment. The thought of a traditional workplace was overwhelming and beyond expectations, given the experiences and trauma they had been through. Dai was given the task as a charity to help these people gain legitimate and meaningful employment. This was a huge ask for a small charity so Dai and a friend set up a small business called Manumit Coffee Roasters which they run on a voluntary basis alongside their full-time employment.[1]

Manumit began in Son Dai's dining room table when he purchased a coffee roaster named Wilber after Wilber Force, the person behind the abolition of slavery movement in the nineteenth century.[2] The success of this home-based enterprise led to Manumit building a coffee roastery in Cardiff which is currently a thriving business aiming to become fully eco-sustainable using recycling packaging where possible.

Manumit functions on three core principles which they make sure that the people who work for them know are genuine and truly implemented – you are safe, you are precious and you are free to dream.

Small Business Enterprise

Manumit began as small business with the sole purpose of creating a working environment that was safe and encouraging for victims of modern-day slavery. A vision that Dai and Nic have created with the input of Esther Hope Gibbs and numerous other unnamed employees.

Offering dignity and hope to survivors of modern slavery through training and employment in a secret coffee roastery (as often employees live in fear of being found

---

1 Insightful and inspired perspectives on Manumit Coffee Roasters were gained from presentations to Cardiff University students by Esther Gibbs and Dai Hankey. Further insights were gained from the radio interview, BBC Radio Wales, All Things Considered. https://www.bbc.co.uk/programmes/m000vvw4
2 https://www.parliament.uk/about/living-heritage/transformingsociety/tradeindustry/slavetrade/over view/wilberforce-makes-the-case/

and returned to slavery), coffee is roasted by people who are now trying to rebuild their lives rebuilding their lives.

Manumit aims to combat slavery at all steps of its coffee production process – sources beans directly from trade with coffee farmers to ensure their coffee is slavery free at source.

People who work for Manumit know as soon as they arrive that three core principles are at the core of the business success:

1. Employees are staff; they work in a safe working environment where they are protected and cared for working with peace of mind, among people who will look after and care for them.

    The building has no signage and the location is shared with very few people. The Manumit team put time and attention into making sure people know they are cared for and looking after those who are struggling, providing space and support not just in the workplace but in wider life.
2. Everyone who walks across the threshold of Manumit is told and made to feel precious. Based on Dai's Christian philosophy every human no matter what walk of life, every single person is precious and will be treated with value and dignity. One of Dai's underlying beliefs, given the trauma and experiences of female modern-day slaves, is that one of the most important things he can do for female Manumit employees is to make sure they have at least one man in their life who cherishes them, honours them and looks after them.
3. Everyone is free to dream, to spread their wings and feel enabled to explore what they want to achieve in life. They do not need to want to work in the coffee industry, but it is the start of something new: new confidence, new skills and a new ability to cope with life outside the horrors of slavery. Everyone is free to dream, spread their wings to explore what they want to do in their lives, not necessarily in the coffee industry but wherever they dream. Manumit is a stepping stone to where they want to be.

An example of the success of this philosophy is *Anne* who is an expert coffee roaster and a talented artist. They have designed Manumit labels, packaging, reusable cups and clothing branding.[3]

Manumit is a non-profit business with Dai not taking a salary and all profits being invested locally, for example in 2021, it donated £28,000 to local slavery charities and organisations.

Coffee (and other products) are sold online to local businesses in bulk (e.g. Cardiff Business School) and to retail outlets across the UK. Their largest retailer to date is the high-end UK retailer Selfridges.[4]

3 https://www.manumitcoffee.co.uk/collections/merch
4 https://www.selfridges.com/GB/en/features/about-us/

Manumit Coffee Roasters Branding (Source: Dai Hankey).

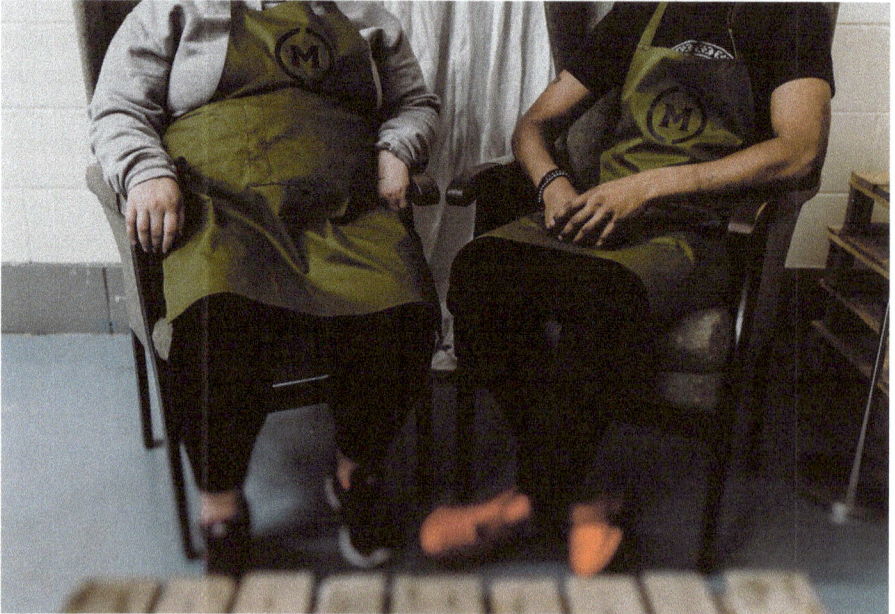

Manumit Coffee Roasters (Source: Dai Hankey).

The Future

As Dai often states, '*Modern slavery is not going away.*' Manumit is set to thrive after surviving the COVID-19 lockdown with the support of the local community and customers, allowing them to continue to provide dignity and hope to survivors of modern slavery by offering training and employment in the coffee roasting industry.

The Goodwash Company

Synopsis

The Goodwash Company began life in Mandy Powell's kitchen, where she used locally sourced, organic, essential oils to create a range of natural hair-, skin- and fur-care products for humans and dogs. The Goodwash Company is not only focused on luxury, sustainable skincare but it also has a social impact. It invests all its profits in local communities and charities and has, so far, Mandy confirmed that so far, they that have contributed £75,000 to local community and social organisations.

The outgoing Future Generations Commissioner for Wales[1] created the 'Future Generations Changemaker 100' list of people making a positive difference to the nation.[2] Mandy Powell and Kelly Davies, co-founders of The Goodwash Company, are listed at number nineteen.

> Kelly and Mandy set up the Goodwash Company, a certified social enterprise that consistently strives to make a difference. Told that creating a high-end, luxury brand with a social conscience would never work, Mandy and Kelly have proved that to be wrong, and are helping to change the world, *one wash at a time*. All sales and fundraising profits from their soaps and other bathing products go to good causes, and social impact is at the heart of everything they do. (Sophie Howe, 2023)

The Goodwash Company is not an extravagant brand. While it offers luxury, high-end products, its unique selling point is its ethical and social impact. The enterprise aims to make a positive impact on the skincare supply chain, including farmers and packaging companies, and on the community in which they trade. It sells skincare products directly to customers through its retail unit and online; it also sells wholesale to retailers, corporate organisations and the luxury hospitality industry.

---

1 https://www.futuregenerations.wales/
2 https://www.futuregenerations.wales/wp-content/uploads/2023/01/FINAL-ENGLISH-Future-Generations-Changemaker-100.pdf

https://doi.org/10.1515/9783110756142-008

Mandy Powell founder of The Goodwash Company (Source: Mandy Powell).

History

The Goodwash Company was founded by Mandy Powell and Kelly Davies, who first met at the Sport Wales Awards. They discovered that, although they had different professional backgrounds, they shared the same life philosophy and ethical business ethos. Mandy, an international hockey and touch-rugby player, had a well-paid, prestigious career working for the pharmaceutical company Pfizer, where she gained a wealth of knowledge and expertise about the science of skincare. Meanwhile, Kelly, a former national and international footballer and chair of the Cymru Football Foundation, brought her social-enterprise expertise to The Goodwash Company during its first three years of trading.

There were also two furry founders – Maisy, a Westie with sensitive skin, and Duffle, a Labradoodle – who were the inspiration for the company's popular Dog Wash.[3]

Small Business Enterprise

The marketing philosophy of The Goodwash Company is based on authenticity, which leads to brand success.

Mandy, like other small business owners, enjoys the benefits of doing what she wants with her brand without the need to seek permission or approval from others. She is empowered to develop the brand as she sees fit. For example, despite receiving advice to the contrary, she made her dogs part of the brand story by taking them to marketing events and festivals, and to the retail unit. This has contributed to the development of good customer relationships with dog lovers (among others), who have bought into the authenticity of the company. Mandy firmly believes in her business philosophy and has not been dissuaded by others questioning her ideas. Thus, she has established a loyal customer following and gained support for the brand.

Small business owners must become experts in all elements of their enterprise, including finance, marketing, packaging, product-production regulations, social media and online sales platforms. The Goodwash Company logo was designed in a London bar by Mandy, together with some friends. Wash Design[4] developed a brand identity for the company that 'reflected their unique aim to provide luxury, organic, cruelty-free bathing products with a social enterprise twist. The final design employed a colour palette, typography and logo that exemplified the luxury, high-end nature of their products while reflecting the Welsh heritage' (Wash Design, 2023). The brand identity is transfer-

---

3 The Goodwash Company Dog Wash is natural, essential-oil fur wash with flea repellent; it is cruelty- and chemical-free and is recommended for sensitive, furry skin.
4 https://www.washdesign.co.uk/

able across print and online media and all other visual representations, such as packaging.

The Goodwash Company produces a luxury, sustainable skincare range, which is designed, manufactured from local organic produce and packaged in Wales. The core product range is essential, skincare with 'no fuss, no floss and no marketing hype' according to the online shop.

Products are sold online and from a retail unit at the Goodsheds community project site on a disused railway line in a regeneration area of Barry, South Wales.[5] The units are housed in 54 repurposed, stacked shipping containers that accommodate local hospitality and small businesses.

Mandy has become a small business role model for women entrepreneurs and has spoken at university events and online lectures, reiterating the message that good entrepreneurs never doubt themselves. Mandy had been told that The Goodwash Company could never succeed as both a luxury and social enterprise, and that a dog wash could not be marketed alongside a human skincare range. However, as she pointed out in a recent podcast,[6] she has proved her critics wrong.

Social-Enterprise Business Philosophy

As a social enterprise, The Goodwash Company works with local suppliers and employs local, disadvantaged people – including long-term unemployed people, individuals with learning difficulties, and people excluded from mainstream society – to help, for example, with labelling and bottling skincare products. There is no marketing department and no distribution centre to receive the orders. These business functions are carried out by Mandy and contracted workers from the local disadvantaged community.

5 https://www.goodshedsbarry.co.uk/
6 https://www.southwales.ac.uk/business-services/usw-exchange-events-membership/developing-en
trepreneurial-women/inspiring-women-wales/episode-3-mandy-powell/

Mandy Powell (Source: Mandy Powell).

The social activities of the company include:

- *Football Association of Wales* – for every bottle of sports body wash or sport lotion sold, the company contributes £3.00 to be reinvested in women and girls' football in Wales.[7]

  Prostate Cymru – the enterprise collaborates with the charity Prostate Cymru to produce a range of skincare with the aim of raising money for and awareness of the disease and saving men's lives.[8] In keeping with Mandy's passion for cycling, to launch the collaboration, she organised a sponsored bike ride from Prostate Cymru's offices to the shop at Goodsheds in Barry.

- *Challenge Wales #oneflameatatime* – in collaboration with the sailing charity Challenge Wales, The Goodwash Company has developed the Conwy candle, with sale proceeds going towards supporting mental health initiatives through education at sea.[9]

Customer loyalty stems from social impact, and the impact of The Goodwash Company is increased by its loyal customers. In Mandy's words, a small enterprise 'finds its people.'

The Future

Customers are conscious of the actions of the brands with which they choose to engage. At the height of the COVID-19 pandemic, some brands were named and shamed for questionable activities during a time of global crisis and showed themselves to be solely profit driven (Maddyness, 2020). Consumers are making purchase choices that have a social impact and The Goodwash Company continues to harness the power of socially conscious consumers. Plans for the future will build on this advancing consumer consciousness with plans to develop the hotel and restaurant range.

References

Howe, S. (2023). https://www.futuregenerations.wales/wp-content/uploads/2023/01/FINAL-ENGLISH-Future-Generations-Changemaker-100.pdf

Maddyness (2020). https://www.maddyness.com/uk/2020/05/13/covid-19-interview-with-mandy-powell-co-founder-the-goodwash-company/

Wash Design. (2023). https://www.washdesign.co.uk/portfolio_page/the-goodwash-company/

---

7 https://goodwash.co.uk/the-goodwash-company-supporting-football-in-wales/ (accessed 5 December 2023).

8 https://www.prostatecymru.com/award-winning-welsh-soap-brand-the-goodwash-company-joins-forces-with-prostate-cymru-for-the-good-cycle/ (accessed 5 December 2023).

9 https://goodwash.co.uk/improve-lives-of-young-people-with-challenge-wales-oneflameatatime/

Modest Trends London

Synopsis

Modest Trends London offers sustainable, affordable, modest fashion – a trend started in 2016 by British Muslim women who were interested in fashion but keen to maintain modesty for religious and personal reasons. Modest fashion was very limited at the time, with women finding it difficult to source clothing that both suited modesty requirements and followed current fashion trends. For example, finding a fashionable, full-length dress with long sleeves and coordinating head scarf was nearly impossible in the UK, where women who dressed modestly tended to wear traditional long, black, cloak-like clothing. However, Rifhat Qureshi had a drive and desire to find modest clothing in bright, colourful, sophisticated, seasonal patterns. She has achieved this through Modest Trends London.

Rifhat Qureshi Founder Modest Trends London (Source: Rifhat Qureshi).

https://doi.org/10.1515/9783110756142-009

History

There are 3.9 million British Muslims in the UK (Office of National Statistics, 2023), whose fashion requirements are frequently misunderstood and misrepresented. Modest Trends London aims to shift the perception that modest fashion simply involves bows and jewellery embellishments to a recognition that it should not be exclusive nor elite but available to women who work, take children to school, go out to eat and go to the gym.

Rifhat is an enterprise educator who is involved with several different community organisations that help educate people, especially women and those from minority groups, with the aim of breaking down social-economic barriers and creating a more equal society. She is an inspirational role model for women entrepreneurs from minority groups.

As the founder of Modest Trends London, Rifhat's mission is to enable women who dress modestly to look great, while looking after the environment and providing opportunities for others through entrepreneurial education. Modest Trends London pledges that for every hijab purchased, they will donate one to charity.

The idea for Modest Trends London developed from a shopping trip Rifhat made while on holiday in Dubai. She noticed a range of different fashion styles not available in the UK and began to think about bringing this modest fashion home to sell. However, turning this idea into reality seemed a remote possibility at the time – possible but with many issues to consider. Rifhat used all her holiday money (from gifts and savings) to buy modest fashion, which she packed in her luggage and brought home to Cardiff with no idea what to do with the range of clothing she now owned.

Rifhat began taking pictures of the clothing and posted them on Facebook. She held a fashion event in the local mosque to test the market, hoping she would, at least, recoup her investment. Indeed, she doubled her money and received a lot of interest from the women in her local community. She then set about sourcing suppliers. This was a new, emerging market with no established suppliers, so she had to establish new supplier links. People in the UK who were operating in the modest-fashion market at the time would fly to Dubai, fill their suitcases with modest fashion and return home to sell the clothes in retail outlets and markets; very few distributors followed structured logistical, supply-chain procedures.

Small Business Enterprise

Rifhat had been exploring entrepreneurship for some time when she launched Modest Fashion London in 2019. Her entrepreneurial journey started in Dubai, where she saw inspirational, modest-fashion clothing that she loved – the sort of clothing she would wear but that was not available in the UK.

Modest Trends London (Source: Rifhat Qureshi).

Rifhat Qureshi (Source: Rifhat Qureshi).

Born in England and raised in Cardiff, Rifhat was unaware of the availability and range of modest fashion outside the UK. She had a passion for fashion from a very young age, reading *Cosmopolitan* to follow the latest fashion trends and being truly fascinated by the magazine. She never thought fashion would become the focus of her first small business enterprise as, although she loved to think about it, she could not imagine selling it – that is, until the trip to Morocco when she started to explore different cultures and places and became inspired by some of the most varied modest fashion available. At the time, Rifhat was not working in modest fashion but was interested in exploring the market possibilities. Several years later, her research resulted in a fashion range for the next generation of Muslim women, which is ethical, socially sourced and built on a platform that will hopefully become a collaborative space for fashion designers and other small business owners.

> Maybe I could start a movement where, rather than it just being modest fashion, we could think about the reputation of the fashion industry and think about how we can maybe make some improvements along the way. So, I started to map out [. . .] what I [really] wanted modest trends to stand for, and [it] came down to being ethical, making sure that I am transparent in my dealings, demonstrating honesty and integrity, [and] applying sustainable business activities; for me, this means making sure I am using sustainable fabric [and] packaging that can be recycled and reused. I recognize that is a big challenge in the fashion industry. (Rifhat Qureshi interview, 2023)

The Modest Trends London Collection

The Modest Trends London collection is functional, attractive and good value for money. The brand's status has rapidly developed among its target market thanks to social influencers and media interest in the movement to empower modest fashionistas.

Modest Trends London first planned to work in collaboration with a design company; however, this company's negative impact on the environment and unsustainable supply chain did not sit well with Rifhat who did not want to contribute to fast fashion (mass market inexpensive clothing). One of her business philosophies is that a brand should contribute positively to society and the environment, and not add to societal or environmental burdens. Modest Trends London was founded on the core proposition that the brand's values must empower women through small business enterprises.

Relationships with Suppliers and Customers

Rifhat found that suppliers were often not totally truthful about or ethical in their sourcing of materials. For example, she found that some suppliers in Turkey and Pakistan, while claiming to source and manufacture locally, were buying from sweatshops in India and flying products around the world under their own brand name.

An organised, regulated supply chain has financial costs that Rifhat was not pre-pared for – for example, costs for delivery and customs paperwork – which she had to pass on to the consumer. This was an experimental, learning stage for the new start-up, and Rifhat decided to invite some potential customers to a meeting where she asked them what type of distribution they wanted: a store, a website or an App. She knew they loved her clothing, but she knew little else about them. During this period, she learnt not to be afraid of sharing her ideas. She had been concerned that people would tell her that her ideas were stupid (and some did); she had also been worried about challenging neg-ative stereotypes of Muslim women. It was only when she started sharing her ideas that opportunities, she had never believed possible started to come her way. For example, when ordering flooring for her new shop, she told the carpet supplier about her plans, and he told her about a sole trader he knew in the northwest of England who owned a small, established, modest-fashion brand that supplied the big fast-fashion market. Rifhat visited the sole trader in Manchester and there she found her supplier. Networking and sharing ideas can lead to longstanding, ethical supplier and customer relationships.

Promotional Innovations

Modest Trends London has achieved an incredible amount of attention in the local and UK modest-fashion industry, cumulating in the opening of a pop-up shop on Ox-ford Street in 2021. Aspect Accelerator[1] provided support for the fledging Modest Trends London, offering the enterprise space to work and publicity opportunities, in-cluding a presentation at TEDx.[2] These opportunities helped develop Rifhat's self-belief, which she considers to be an integral part of personal, self-development.

Support for Women Entrepreneurs from Minority Groups

Coming from a family of entrepreneurs, Rifhat was the first person in her extended family to go to university. Her family admires her work: she is the clever one who gets to travel to different places to work – the professional. She began her career at a local collective working for the Prince's Trust until, 10 years later, she joined Cardiff University as a student union personal development officer, where she coordinated student development programmes and enterprise education until she left to focus on Modest Trends London in 2019.

Mother to three teenagers, Rifhat has a busy life. Her children inspire and moti-vate her to succeed – she is their role model – and she feels that she has an opportu-

---

1 https://aspect.ac.uk/funded-project/arc-accelerator-phase-2-accelerator-for-shape-ventures/
2 https://www.ted.com/talks/rifhat_qureshi_self_belief_and_how_it_can_change_your_world

nity to empower other women in her life. An objective of Modest Trends London is to facilitate equality for women, especially those from areas of the world where it is not a given. As the founder of the enterprise, Rifhat looks for ways in which women from minority groups can empower themselves. She believes there is a strong connection between empowerment and women being able to work for themselves through small business enterprises.

Rifhat's success has enabled her to support female entrepreneurs, in partnership with the charity Assadaqaat Community Finance,[3] which provides enterprise education, interest-free micro loans and mentoring for women who have innovative, creative ideas but no understanding of how to launch a new business start-up. Rifhat believes that the main reasons women do not start a business are fear and lack of access to finance or networks for advice and support.

This success has led to her partnership with the charity Water Aid. The impact of water on women in least-developed societies is a largely unrecognised problem. Women in these countries spend a lot of time going back and forth trying to source clean water throughout both day and night. These women also suffer when they have their periods as there is a lack of suitable sanitation. These and other ramifications of the lack of clean water led Rifhat to start thinking about how she and Modest Trends London could support the clean-water campaign. In Islam, water is a gift, giving life and providing opportunities. However, not everyone has the luxury of being able to access clean water. By partnering with Water Aid, Modest Trends London is working to provide women and girls with access to clean water, sanitation and hygiene resources to help them reach their full potential.

The Future

Rifhat aims to make modest fashions available to women in her community and across the UK. She plans to grow the Modest Trends London brand to reach a wider target audience and empower women to wear what makes them feel comfortable and fashionable. Her aims extend to creating employment opportunities for Muslim women in her community, thus, not only empowering fashion but also empowering women to achieve their aspirational goals. Rifhat, with her inspirational fashion insight, is an inspiration to her children, her family and her wider community.

Reference

Office of National Statistics. (2023). https://www.ons.gov.uk/peoplepopulationandcommunity/

3 https://www.assadaqaatcommunityfinance.co.uk/Communityfinance/

Part Two: **Community and Society Benefits:
Educating, Informing, Changing
Behaviours**

The Lion Treorchy (Source: Adrian Emmett).

Cafe Môr Freshwater Bay West beach (Source: Jonathan Williams).

https://doi.org/10.1515/9783110756142-010

Part Two offers the reader stories of six small business enterprises that benefit society by educating, informing and changing behaviours, embracing their community through disruptive and creative approaches to their branding and consumer engagement.

The Lion not only offers sport, food, drink and entertainment, but it is a community hub that extends to supporting local people, social groups and the wider society.

HiR Dining is a small restaurant on the outskirts of San Jose in Costa Rica, offering an intimate jungle culinary experience hosted in the chef's home.

Greenstream Flooring CIC was established to redirect used flooring from landfill, providing training and employment, and low-cost flooring to those in need in the local community.

Teesandcoffee was a small business created by two student friends which sourced and produced sustainable streetwear and biodegradable cups.

Forest Green Rovers Football Club is the world's first carbon-neutral football club.

Pembrokeshire Beachfood Company began life as the seafood snack bar Café Môr on the beach in Freshwater Bay West where surfers queued to enjoy food items made using local ethically sourced seaweed.

The Lion – The Heart of Treorchy

This chapter is based on a case study developed from ideas and research generated by Brodi Parfitt during her undergraduate studies at Cardiff Business School.

> "Adrian (Emmett) has over ten years' experience in the regeneration of post-industrial towns and was the driving-force in the transformation of Treorchy from a left behind place into a thriving valleys community." https://www.nearmenow.eu/#partners

Synopsis

Innovative and creative entrepreneurship is epitomised by Adrian Emmett, the landlord of The Lion – more than a pub – at the heart of the Welsh valley's village of Treorchy, awarded the winner of the Community Hero at the Great British Pub Awards 2022 (Stonegate Group, 2022).

The synopsis of Adrian Emmett is captured in this statement by the Community Hero awarding body:

> Adrian has built up a huge community presence, supports numerous local causes and is always finding ways to help and make a positive impact within the local community. The pub has long been the centre point for successful high street initiatives such as the Christmas Parade and together with his team partnerships have been forged with local schools and charities; community groups and festivals have been supported. Projects such as the new multi-purpose "Live at the Box" library and reading red phone box, and the "Green Valley" sustainable fruit and veg shop, have been undertaken providing services way beyond that of a typical pub. The Lion received a special visit in July 2022, during a tour of Wales by non-other than His Majesty King Charles III and Her Majesty The Queen Consort, who stopped by to meet Adrian and the team, with the now King even pouring a pint behind the bar.[1]

---

1 https://www.stonegategroup.co.uk/press/treorchy-pub-is-a-winner-at-this-years-great-british-pub-awards/

https://doi.org/10.1515/9783110756142-011

Adrian Emmett (Source: Adrian Emmett).

History

Adrian Emmett grew up in the small town of Treorchy in the Welsh Rhondda Valley, a town that is occupied by 6,000 residents and was once the thriving coal capital of the world. Since then, the coal industry has disappeared, leaving Treorchy fighting poverty and an increasing lifeless community. He decided to leave the town at the age of eighteen to attend the University of Bristol to study Business and Information Systems, succumbing to social pressures to get a degree and expectations to be academically ambitious, social norms at the time urged people to move away from the town which led to a depletion of talent within the community – Treorchy's future looked bleak and grey. However, after years of experience working in the bar and nightclub industry, travelling all over the country, working in Nottingham, Gloucester, Coventry, Cardiff, Glasgow and Wigan, Adrian decided to go home in 2011 with a fresh outlook on the town and its future. Adrian bought closed and rundown The Lion located in the heart of the High Street and made it his mission to make the small town where he grew up innovative and special once again.

Themes

Adrian's decision to take ownership of The Lion led to the creation of a community hub within the village of Treorchy which pushed the boundaries of expected social norms of what is perceived to be a traditional pub (pub is a traditional British public drinking establishment licenced to serve alcoholic drinks to be consumed on the premises). Initially, Adrian was faced with the task of refurbishing the dilapidated pub that was seen merely as a *'local boozer for old men with red noses'* (Davies-Lewis, 2017). According to Adrian, British pubs tended to have a bad reputation, known to be places that thrived on excessive alcohol consumption and antisocial behaviour, while the landlord was known merely as the person who assisted these bad behaviours in coming to fruition. This was a narrative that Adrian wanted to change with his vision of what The Lion could be and what it could mean for the community. It was important for Adrian to offer more than just a pub where people could come to drink. Recognising the importance of diversifying his offering (Davies-Lewis, 2017), he wanted to create a sanctuary for everyone in the community, catering to every age and every need. This allowed Adrian to view matters through a clearer lens. Rather than offering what was expected of a public house owner and fulfilling the bare minimum of the pub's potential, he saw an opportunity for change. It is important to understand the motivations that drive individuals such as Adrian towards becoming creative entrepreneurs – Adrian's drive is the prosperity of Treorchy and its community; this has always been his main goal.

The Lion Treorchy (Source: Adrian Emmett).

King Charles and Queen Camilla visit The Lion (Source: Adrian Emmett).

Small Business Enterprise

Adrian explored several strategic initiatives to help Treorchy reach its fullest potential. In the hands of Adrian Emmett, The Lion has become the hub of Treorchy. The pub offers high-quality food, drink and an all-inclusive atmosphere, allowing everyone, including families with small children to feel welcome. It was important to Adrian that The Lion diversify offerings to the wider Treorchy community; this led to the launch of events and experiences in The Lion for the wider community, including Afternoon Teas, Royal Ascott Ladies Day, sporting events, weekly live entertainment including quizzes, charity events and live music. The Lion hosts five yearly festivals with a plethora of artists and DJs who come to perform in the pub's large outdoor area. Adrian creates event in The Lion and the village every celebratory holiday, dressing up and hanging, and has instigated village celebrations for occasions throughout the year, from Valentine's Day to St David's Day, to Halloween to St Patrick's Day. Adrian has converted a second-floor storage room into a comedy club/theatre area that can hold up to 70 people, offering quality acts as well as a space for school children to rehearse or for locals to hire for meetings or discussion groups. The Lion offers a place where everyone can feel a sense of belonging and togetherness at every point throughout the year, whatever the occasion. Adrian's ability to capitalise on inclusivity and his talent to bring a community together led to The Lion winning numerous awards including Best Pub in the UK, Best Community Pub in Wales and Best Sports Pub in Wales.

Adrian's capacity to incorporate creativity and innovation into his entrepreneurial role knows no bounds. Aside from The Lion, Adrian injects himself into every aspect of Treorchy's community. He strives to build partnerships and links with every business, without seeking any means of personal gain. This includes working with the police force, to have security and assist with traffic for the local school's prom and the fire brigade, to ensure safety measures are in place for the yearly firework display and to help with building the floats for the Christmas parade each year. Adrian is at the centre of every one of Treorchy's events, ensuring that everything runs smoothly giving funding and his expertise and his time to ensure success.

Community Involvement

Adrian works with local primary and comprehensive schools in the Rhondda Valley; one of the successful projects created an attendance challenge for pupils that offers prizes to students whose attendances are over 98 percent. Adrian is committed to enhancing community life in Treorchy. He has assembled groups of over 100 people to participate in community clean-up projects.

Adrian's community involvement peaks during the approach to Christmas each year. He arranges the delivery and decoration of the town Christmas tree as well as brass bands and choirs that perform over the holiday. He also coordinates the yearly Christmas jumper competition and the Christmas shop window competition, inviting judges from Cardiff University, local businesses, schools and charities, bringing all the small businesses in the town together to create a sense of belonging, while making the town itself look beautiful, welcoming tourists and Christmas shoppers from far and wide.

As a small local business, it is difficult to stay afloat, especially during today's economic climate. So, it is not surprising that Adrian received some initial pushback from business owners who do not have the resources to take part in such town events, parades and competitions. However, due to Adrian's excellent communication skills and delivery of the community message, he was able to galvanise the people of the town, getting everyone involved to achieve a common goal. He made business owners realise that their involvement will help create a sense of place for locals and tourists alike, and that town residents will be proud of where they come from. Adrian's ability to diversify common notions and his focus on adding value to the community instead of purely making money, has prompted tourists to travel up the valley towards Treorchy, as opposed to in the past, where they would generally migrate down the valley towards Cardiff to get to bigger shops and towns. Adrian has been a catalyst in changing the perception of his small town, even forcing train schedules to adapt to Treorchy's newfound influx of tourism.

Adrian is the Chair of the Treorchy Chamber of Trade, growing its members from 30 to 120 since he has been in management. As Chair, he launched the 'Visit Treorchy' brand, including its own website and social media platforms, to engage with both locals and tourists to promote every wonderful thing that Treorchy has to offer. Following this, Adrian applied for the Champion High Street of Great Britain Awards, with Treorchy's dismal past, it's hard to believe that such a town would even be in contention for such a prestigious award; however, the town was shortlisted alongside two others. The day that the judges came to visit Treorchy to judge the winner, the Rhondda was issued an amber weather warning due to heavy rain, because of this, trains were cancelled, roads were closed and town decorations were destroyed. In the face of adversity, Adrian rallied the entire community together to create a day to remember, which included dance troops, market stalls and flash mob of Treorchy's male voice choir that performed Calon Lan in The Lion. The flash mob was recorded on a local's mobile phone and the video went viral, receiving over 257,000 views. It is interesting to note that the flash mob was also professionally filmed by a paid cameraman, but this social media post received only 3,000 views. These figures support the power of community and how Adrian was able to ward off inhibitors to innovation and create a unity within the community. This also supports Adrian's belief that marketing a brand is not about forcing it onto people or artificially creating content through external sources, it is about user-generated content and helping people to fall in love with who you are and what you do. From this, brand loyalty will automatically follow and grow organically. The success of the day and the perseverance of Adrian Emmett contributed to Treorchy becoming the 2019 Great British High Street Award winner.

Adrian thrives in the face of adversity. This was evident following the devastation caused by Storm Dennis after their Great British High Street win. Adrian's ability to cope with the damaging effects of the flood, as well as the restrictions placed upon society because of the COVID-19 pandemic exemplifies this. After fixing the damages caused by the flood, Adrian set out to overcome the challenges placed upon the town because of the pandemic. The outbreak of COVID-19 and its consequential lockdown required Adrian (as well as many other pub landlords) to abandon countless kegs of beer and large quantities of food, as well as being forced to shut The Lion doors to the public for the foreseeable future. Once again, Adrian overcame what was seen to many as unsurmountable. In the wake of the pandemic, Adrian launched Mypubshop outside The Lion. He sold fresh fruit and vegetables to members of the public and delivered them to NHS staff and to those who were most vulnerable. He didn't stop there, after receiving a grant of £15,000 from a local wind farm organisation, he put together COVID safety packs for every business in Treorchy and for neighbouring towns. Each pack consisted of visors, safety screens, hand sanitisers, social distance floor stickers and posters. From this, he created the We Are COVID Ready campaign, putting together How It Works guides for each local business. He presented the universal safety measures that had been put in place by the town to the Welsh Government. As a result, both the Welsh Government and countless news reporters devoted entire news coverage segments and social media videos to The Lion, demonstrating to the rest of the country how things should and could be done with a proactive leader and the cohesion of a community. Due to the chaos and uncertainty that the pandemic has caused, and the public's expectation of disruption and changing norms, it has perhaps been easier for Adrian to implement new, innovative schemes that dispute the status quo, allowing Adrian the freedom to push the boundaries of traditional pub landlord behaviours.

The Future

Adrian's future as an entrepreneur sees many aspects of creativity, through his vision to digitise Treorchy's high street (https://www.nearmenow.eu), a project launched in 2022 which aims to combat the *retail monster that is Amazon* bringing small business in Treorchy onto one shopping App, funded and supported by the Welsh Government and Cardiff University.[2] This type of forward thinking and openness to progression is how the modern world will be able to prosper in years to come, even in the face of adversity. Entrepreneurial leaders like Adrian form the heart of our communities, bringing people together in adversity and celebration.

References

Davies-Lewis, T. (2017). The small village pub that's just been named the best sports bar in Wales. *Wales Online*. https://www.walesonline.co.uk/whats-on/food-drink-news/lion-treorchy-been-named-best-13609532

Stonegate Group. (2022). https://www.stonegategroup.co.uk/press/treorchy-pub-is-a-winner-at-this-years-great-british-pub-awards/

---

2 Adrian Emmett guest lecturer, Cardiff Business School, October 2020.

HiR Dining

The name 'HiR' represents the integration of opposites. HiR Fine Dining is the creation of Mercedes Noam Kostucki, an artist, entrepreneur and creator. HiR Fine Dining combines refined and luxurious food with a rustic and casual family style environment.

HiR Fine Dining is an intimate three hours dining experience a maximum of 12 guests per night. Dinners take place at Mercedes Noam's home and guests are seated all together along the same table. If you chose to join this culinary adventure, you will be taken on journey that integrates opposites. (Mercedes Noam Kostucki, 2023. https://www.elmundodenoam.com/hirfinedining)

Synopsis

Mercedes Noam Kostucki is a Belgian entrepreneur who has lived and travelled all over the world, and they currently reside in Costa Rica. Mercedes is a gender-fluid fine dining experience Chef.

Mercedes Noam has taken advantage of adversities and is very talented at turning problems into opportunities. Mercedes's life in Costa Rica began as life coach, working with entrepreneurs from all over the world helping them raise money for their start-ups, helping them grow and develop. After buying a piece of land in Costa Rica to open a coaching retreat; many problems thwarted the development plans including poor internet connection which hindered the delivery of online coaching sessions. Mercedes had two choices: give up on the piece of land in Costa Rica as solving the internet problems was not realistic or take on a new challenge.

Mercedes thought hard about what to do next and realised they had always loved cooking, but not working as a chef in a restaurant kitchen which they felt is very hierarchical where you are stuck in a little hot, hectic room working unsociable hours, never seeing people – a job that kills all the fun of food. The next step of this wonderful entrepreneur's life was to create organised dinners in their home, with no menu and surprise cooking of little taster dishes.

And so began HiR dining which offers four to six diners to travel to Mercedes's house, a 30-minute drive from the closest town for dinner cooked in full view of the diners and served by Mercedes using only local ingredients. Mercedes is the physical representation of the restaurant.[1]

---

[1] https://www.youtube.com/watch?v=O81tRd-E3FM&t=68s

https://doi.org/10.1515/9783110756142-012

Mercedes Noam Kostucki HiR Dining (Source: Mercedes Noam Kostucki).

History

Mercedes Noam Kostucki discusses the history of their life in a beautifully written autobiography, *Transgression: My very public journey into becoming a (wo)man*, published in 2021. A brief summary of their career history follows:

Mercedes began their professional life in May 2006 as a venture management graduate trainee in Singapore with McKinsey consultants. They were told by line managers that you're *smart but you either need a university degree from a good university or you need to act like you have one.* That's when they decided to get a short haircut, buy a suit and fit in. Much cheaper and faster than another three or more years locked up in an academic jail.

By January 2007, having delivered various conferences all over the world for AIE-SEC,[2] Mercedes moved to Warsaw to live with a girl they met at the Slovakia conference; the career plan was to start a training and coaching company. Several barriers prohibited this plan – they were illegally residing in Poland, they did not speak a word of Polish, they had no money and no University education. Mercedes spent hours calling companies and going to meetings to sell training and coaching services but was always turned down with the helpful suggestion, *'if you don't speak Polish, all you can do is teach English.'* Within months Mercedes spoke fluent English.

In September 2008 Mercedes returned to London just as the financial crisis was at its worst and became a Fundraising Training Consultant for the Directory of Social Change.[3] Once again accepting another job they did not know how to do; they never lied; they simply explaining I do not know what I am doing but I will learn, and they did – going on to earn the accolade of one of the best trainers in the organisation providing over one hundred days of training to young people.

In March of 2009, an old friend approached Mercedes as he was slightly lost after recently graduating – they started Seeducation, a social enterprise that aimed to mentor people who wanted to start small business for a percentage of forthcoming profits.

Seeducation led to Mercedes being invited to give a TEDx in Warsaw talk in 2010, *'When selfishness is a good reason to co-operate.'*[4] A second TEDx invite followed in 2011, *'Making money from doing good'*[5] following the success of these TECx talks, Mercedes published a book, *You are your brand!* (Kostucki, 2011).

Life was going well until April 2012 when Seeducation lost six potential clients over 3 days. With no income and feeling alone and devastated and alone Mercedes spent the weekend editing notes and to create 'clarity in my head', this draft became the second to be published before they reached the age of 26 years old – *Compendium*

2 https://aiesec.org/about-us
3 https://www.dsc.org.uk/
4 https://www.youtube.com/watch?app=desktop&v=VJWLn90XqVQ
5 https://www.youtube.com/watch?v=2gRaHyHJjrg

of business beliefs: Understand how perception affects your important business deci-sions (Kostucki, 2012).

In 2012, after the collapse of Seeducation, Mercedes went back to New York, where they were pleasantly surprised by the inventiveness of the food, and started work at a headhunting firm which only lasted for two short months as the partners had a major falling out resulting in a terrible working environment. This led to another move, to Maryland, USA which was a short stay due to the lack of work and visa issues.

After getting married in 2014, Mr and Mrs Kostucki travelled to Costa Rica for the very first time, deciding it was the 'happiest place in the world'. Without a visa to travel to the American home of the new Mrs Kostucki, Mercedes rented an Airbnb on the beach which is where the online coaching business began.

Small Business Enterprise

By 2016, Mercedes dreamed of creating a coach retreat centre in Costa Rica, creating a business plan, searching for land, constructing a building, seeking investors. This is not developed as planned – poor internet connection, lack of infrastructures and in-vestors not delivering on promises.

Mercedes closed down the coaching business and focused on a lifelong fantasy to open a fine-dining establishment – HiR Fine Dining. Having always loved cooking and needing a stopgap until the coaching business could be restarted, Mercedes created the fine dining experience HiR, converting a rural shack into a restaurant. HiR is a meta-phor Mercedes uses to explain 'him' and 'her' and combined them to make it HiR.

HiR Fine Dining, Unnamed Road, Provincia de Guanacaste, Costa Rica

In Mercedes's words –

> the vague address says it all: this restaurant is quite literally in the middle of the Costa Rican jungle. In one of the more peculiar set-ups on this list, guests listen to the sound of surrounding monkeys while tucking into Japanese French fusion food that one TripAdvisor reviewer com-pares to that of a fancy 5 star restaurant. There's no real menu, but a seven-course tasting menu costs $75 per person and is curated by owner and chef Mercedes Noam. The trilingual ceviche is a show-stopping dish. (Kostuski 2021)

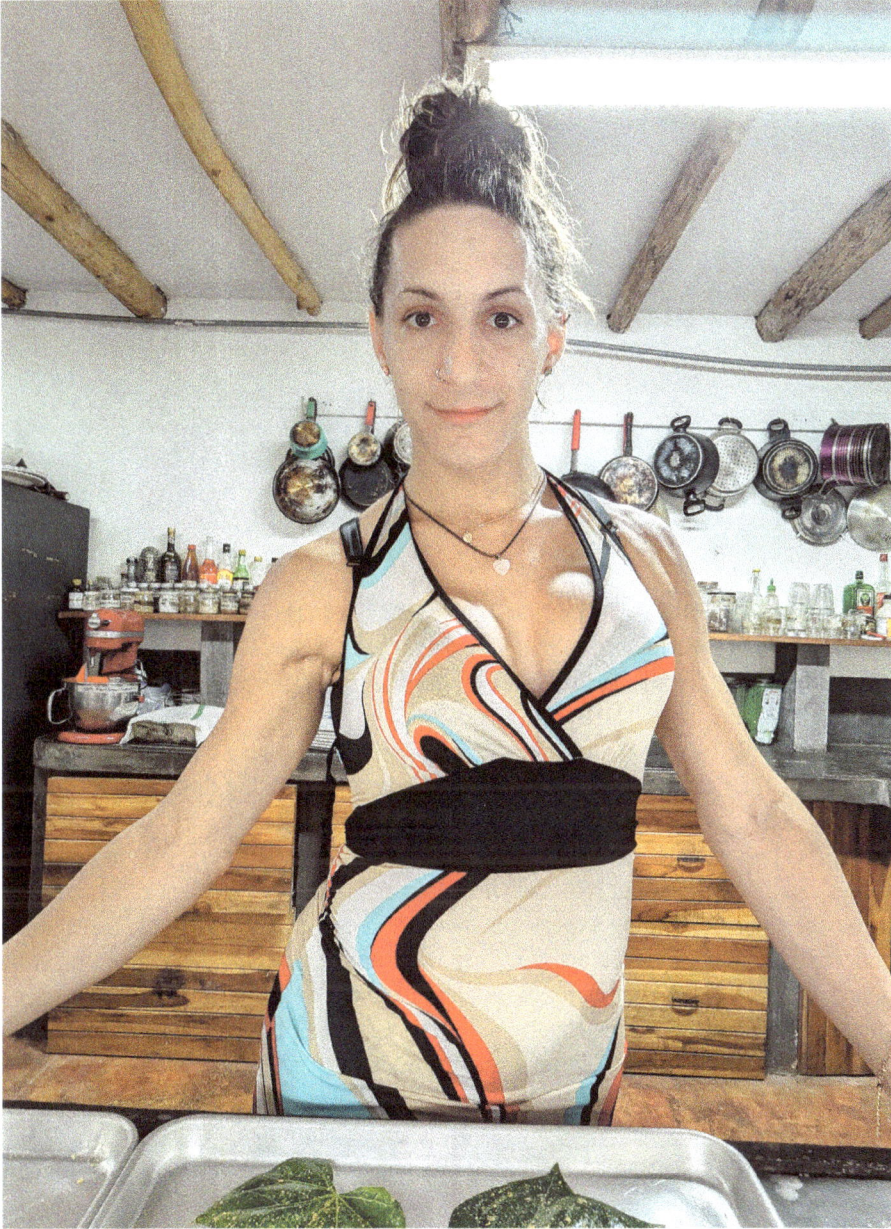

Mercedes Noam Kostucki (Source: Mercedes Noam Kostucki).

HiR Dining (Source: Mercedes Noam Kostucki).

Within 5 months, HiR was rated on Tripadvisor OpenTable as one of *25 dishes to travel around the world for out of 40,000 restaurants.* The restaurant quickly became very popular and within 2 years it was ranked as the number one restaurant in the province on Tripadvisor.[6]

The HiR dig experience involves visiting Mercedes's house and interacting with them while they cook dinner for guests. Mercedes loves talking directly with people, the only person who works at HiR Fine Dining where customers are invited to their home. The only way to book for dinner at HiR Fine Dining is to have a conversation with Mercedes – no online reservation system or texting – customers must speak to Mercedes about the dining experience, availability, dietary restrictions, transportation, wine and payment method – nothing about dining at HiR is mainstream or automated. Before a reservation is confirmed and payment accepted, Mercedes calls every guest to talk about the dining experience, dietary restrictions and transportation.

The success of HiR Fine Dining is that the dining experience creates memories that last for a lifetime, guest have shared stories over and over again on social media.[7]

The HiR Fine Dining experience is an intimate dining experience in Mercedes' home. The restaurant is open to 12 people a night who get to sit beside the kitchen watching the chef cooking and while talking and sharing stories. Everything is sourced, prepared and cooked by Mercedes who also services and clears up after the evening.

---

6 https://www.tripadvisor.com/Restaurant_Review-g7290580-d11875840-Reviews-HiR_Fine_Dining-Pinilla_Tamarindo_Province_of_Guanacaste.html

7 For example https://www.elmundodenoam.com/fine-dining-food-gallery

Promotional Innovation

HiR is promoted by social media and word of mouth. Within a few weeks of launching HiR dining on TikTok, the restaurant reached 30,000 followers with HiR cooking experience videos gaining 200,000 views and 500,000 video likes.

During the first year of launch, Mercedes learnt how to cook and create a unique dining experience. First-time customers think they are going to HiR for dinner, to eat good food; there is so much more than eating at HiR. This is reflected in the cost-free social media promotion provided by customers.

The Future

Mercedes is a positive presence and influencer in their community, as well as HiR; they are a mentor to entrepreneurs, creator and humans; they have a fashion brand Transgression Design.[8] Mercedes currently has plans to expand HiR and is working towards opening an Airbnb to allow travellers to stay and experience the restaurant and its location for longer than an evening dining experience.

References

Kostucki, N. (2011). *You are your brand*. Self-published.

Kostucki, N. (2012). *Compendium of business beliefs: Understand how perception affects your important business decision*. Self-published.

Kostuski, N. (2021). *Transgression: My very public journey into becoming a (wo)man*. Marina London (Ed.), Eabha Strong-Wright (Illustrator), Jorge Madrigal Ygalde (Photographer). Self-published. ISBN 13-979-8721884849.

---

8 https://www.elmundodenoam.com/transgressiondesign

Greensteam Flooring CIC

This chapter is based on a case study developed from ideas and research generated by Lucie Collins during her undergraduate studies at Cardiff Business School.

Synopsis

Ellen Petts is a powerful, innovative and creative entrepreneur who created the social enterprise Greenstream Flooring CIC, which she founded after a conversation with a mutual friend in a bar who happened to work for a large flooring manufacturer. Greenstream Flooring CIC's values and philosophy rested on the desire to maximise social and community benefit from the reuse and sales of flooring in the UK. Based in Rhondda Cynon Taff they supported hundreds of volunteers and training placements for the long-term unemployed and socially disadvantaged, engaging them in their circular model enterprise (Social Enterprise UK, 2022).

Ellen Petts founder of Greenstream Flooring (Source: Ellen Petts).

https://doi.org/10.1515/9783110756142-013

History

After graduating Ellen spent over 10 years working in waste management strategy and community-based sustainable waste management organisations (Social Enterprise UK, 2022), Ellen believed there was a gap in the market for social enterprises that reuse flooring in response to the large number of carpet tiles being wasted and sent to landfill (Greenstream Flooring CIC, 2022). Ellen's *not-for-profit* philosophy is deeply embedded in her work-life values; being diagnosed with leukaemia at twenty-three had a huge impact on her value of life, leading her to believe that health and fulfilment are more important than financial gain (Business Wales, 2022). Ellen had the determination and trust in her circular economy idea, a key attribution of a social entrepreneur. Greenstream Flooring CIC progressed from just a '*good idea*' to being a multi-award winning social enterprise; they employed nine staff in two warehouses and provided flooring and flooring-reuse services across South Wales and London (Business Wales, 2022). Ellen Petts had a clear vision of Greenstream's potential business mission and values; she was able to apply her creative and innovative approaches to an environmental and social need.

Greenstreaming Flooring (Source: Ellen Petts).

Greenstreaming Flooring Warehouse (Source: Ellen Petts).

Theme

Greenstream Flooring CIC adopted a very creative approach to its business and purpose, implanting marketing strategies. Creativity is important for an individual who chooses the life of an entrepreneur, and creativity separates entrepreneurs from other business professionals. (Birdthistle, 2008). Ellen demonstrates creativity in her strategic approach from changing the flooring market to her employees' policies, taking and implementing social values very seriously – Ellen empowered her team members to be part of the business and to be involved in the decisions that affected them and the company's future (Greenstream Flooring CIC, 2022), employee inclusion was a key part of becoming a successful entrepreneur.

Small Business Enterprise

It is important to know exactly what you are setting out to achieve when becoming a social entrepreneur and that you are passionate about it. An important characteristic for an entrepreneur is their value of achievement over money. Ellen has maintained this not-for-profit philosophy – Greenstream Flooring CIC was a social enterprise created for the benefit of others and not simply for financial gain. Ellen had worked 10 years previously in waste strategy management and community-based sustainable waste management and has over 20 years of experience in resource recovery (Social Enterprise UK, 2022). A key to Greenstream's success is that Ellen is personally highly committed to making a social difference through her business.

Ellen was very emotionally invested in Greenstream Flooring CIC. She values the smaller things in life and is not motivated by making a financial profit – rather it's more important to her to achieve social and environmental value. Ellen is an inspirational social entrepreneur. Greenstream Flooring CIC not only offered a sustainable circular economy product and service that disrupts the linear consumption pattern, but it also offered local work-disadvantaged individuals employability programme that provided participants with a work-related confidence-building pathway in a circular/regenerative work-base (Greenstream Flooring CIC, 2022). The company's employability programmes aimed to encourage the wider community to gain life and work skills, making them employees of the future. This emotional investment was implemented through the offering of different employability programmes to local work-disadvantaged residents to train reuse sorters, flooring cutters and fitters. Through this policy, Greenstream not only reused flooring waste but also created social value across the wider community.

Innovation and creative social entrepreneurship are powerful in the current ecologically conscious business world. Becoming a social entrepreneur requires more than having a plan and pitching it to investors, suppliers and consumers. It demands entrepreneurs to be innovative, creative and emotionally able to stand out from the crowd. This was clearly demonstrated by Greenstream, through their ability to keep in line with the purpose of the business and Greenstream who created a very successful social enterprise that clearly delivered extensive social value for the local community while remaining sustainable and profitable.

The Product and Service

Greenstream's strategic approach took an innovative tactic towards the market; they are paid to take care of unwanted flooring usually from large organisations undergoing wide-scale refurbishments; the team cleaned, sorted and graded the collected tiles A–D (Greenstream Flooring CIC, 2022), with Grade A being used tiles but with no sign of wear, marks, indents or fading and Grade D being tiles that show obvious signs of wear and tear (Greenstream Flooring, 2022). They were the only flooring company known to take this approach to used flooring, with regular competitors in the local market not offering upcycled products.

Greenstream recognises and takes advantage of the amount of post-consumer commercial flooring waste and the need to change customers' attitudes and buying behaviour in a circular economy. The post-consumer commercial carpet offered to commercial customers by Greenstream Flooring allowed customers to make a zero embodied carbon choice while supporting the social impact that Greenstream delivers. This strategic approach offers different cost levels to customers who may be driven by price rather than perfection in the product. Customers included the Public Health Wales, a number of Welsh local authorities, the NSW in Wales and Cardiff University, who were all keen to reduce the carbon impact of work done in the built environment within their circular renovation projects.

Another important part of Greenstream's operation was/is the provision of flooring directly from the warehouse to local social housing tenants who could otherwise not afford to cover the floors in their homes. Greenstream Flooring also held donation days on the last Friday of each month which allowed particular groups and individuals in acute need to visit the warehouse and collect free reused carpet tiles. As no social housing landlord, pre-WHQS had an obligation to provide flooring for tenants. The majority of those benefiting from the Donation Days were living with bare concrete or floorboarded floors only. This dual innovative approach involved customers paying for the service and the materials they can afford and being offered free product if they cannot.

The Future

Ellen is an innovator, and she has applied a creative destructive approach towards the flooring market, with sustainability at the core of all the products and services, offerings providing a zero-waste management service by diverting commercial carpet tiles otherwise going to landfill from offices, banks and commercial premises to a second life. She has changed people's lives.

While at Greenstream, Ellen was also a leading advocate in Wales for social procurement and the green agenda more generally. She was part of many relevant strategic alliance groups related to social enterprise, foundation economy and social procurement.

References

Birdthistle, N. (2008). An examination of tertiary students' desire to find an enterprise. *Education + Training*, *50*(7), 552–567.

Business Wales. (2022). Ellen Petts, Greenstream Flooring CIC. https://businesswales.gov.wales/bigideas/profile/ellen-petts

Greenstream Flooring CIC. (2022). *About Us*. https://www.findcarpettiles.co.uk

Social Enterprise UK. (2022). *Ellen Petts*. https://www.socialenterprise.org.uk/social-enterprise-futures/speakers/ellen-petts/

Zimmer T., N. Scarborough and Wilson, S. (2008). *Essentials of Entrepreneurship and Small Business Management*, 5th Edition, Prentice-Hall, Upper Saddle River, 2008.

Tees and Coffee

Synopsis

Tees and Coffee was a socially conscious, small enterprise start-up owned and managed by two young students. Pushpit Bhardwaj and Isaac Greaves[1] are entrepreneurs who first met at school when they were matched as partners after entering the Peter Symonds College (a UK further education/sixth-form college in Winchester) Young Enterprise Competition. Pushpit recently graduated from King's College London, and Isaac is studying architecture and engineering at the Bartlett School of Architecture. Tees and Coffee began trading in 2018 as a Young Enterprise Competition college project in which students were tasked with setting up a new business start-up.[2]

Theme

The underlying drive behind Tees and Coffee was the two young, inspirational entrepreneurs who developed the brand, both working to spread the word of sustainable fashion among their student peers and the wider UK university community. A unique factor in this sustainable business was the resilience of these two young student innovators. They sourced sustainable, recycled materials, marketed a product with no budget and stitched logos onto T-shirts and hoodies between lectures and assignments. They lived with boxes of product piled high in their small London student accommodation, packaging and posting orders themselves.

---

1 Pushpit Bhardwaj: https://www.linkedin.com/in/pushpitbhardwaj/?originalSubdomain=uk
   Isaac Greaves: https://www.linkedin.com/in/isaac-greaves-b8676316b/?originalSubdomain=uk
2 Teesandcoffee.com

https://doi.org/10.1515/9783110756142-014

Isaac Greaves (Source: Isaac Greaves).

Pushpit Bhardwaj (Source: Isaac Greaves).

Small Business Enterprise

The *tees element* of Tees and Coffee were the T-shirts, hoodies and sweatshirts made from recycled plastic bottles and organic cotton, which were designed, sourced and distributed by Pushpit and Isaac. Organic cotton was used when recycled plastic bottles were not available in sufficient quantities, offering the brand a natural, non-chemical alternative. Pushpit and Isaac's aim was to make something useful from an abundant waste product in the consumer market, instead of disposing of it in the oceans. Tees and Coffee sourced recycled fabric and organic cotton from two producers based in South Asia who have a good record of environmental, social, human and economic sustainability while also being involved in local community, social and educational programmes with their employees. This was the core philosophy of the Tees and Coffee T-shirts, hoodies and sweatshirts, with all products being certified by the Fair Wear Foundation.[3]

The *coffee element* of Tees and Coffee was not the drink itself but a range of re-usable, biodegradable coffee cups. Single-use coffee cups cannot be recycled because of the plastic lining required to make the cup leakproof, so switching to a re-usable cup helps eliminate waste. Many re-usable cups are made of hard plastic, but Tees and Coffee cups are made of biodegradable wheat straw, which breaks down naturally on a compost heap within 3–4 years. The cup was ergonomically designed with practical features, including effective insulation and a fully drip-proof lid. They were transported over land to reduce their carbon footprint. Tees and Coffee supported several sustainable campaigns, including a tree-planting subscription service and Black Lives Matter.[4]

When Isaac and Pushpit entered their further-education college's young enterprise competition, they were Belbin-matched[5] and put in a team together. They were both drawn to this extra-curricular project as they thought it would be beneficial to use their spare time at college to develop a new business start-up and make money out of it. Tees and Coffee grew from this seed when Isaac and Pushpit participated in various activities run by the college's young enterprise team, including mentoring and giving a pitch presentation.

After leaving further education in 2020, Isaac and Pushpit decided to continue working on their new business. During COVID-19 lockdowns, they spent time working on ideas for new hoodie and T-shirt designs and creating social media content. Their designs included the Black Lives Matter collection, catchy logos and face masks. They both learnt to sew, so they could not only design the range but also make it themselves. They took a break from running the start-up when they started university but were soon drawn back to create designs that represented young people, which led to the development of the Golden Days collection.

---

3 https://www.fairwear.org/
4 https://blacklivesmatter.com/
5 https://www.belbin.com/

In 2021, in the second year of their university studies, Pushpit and Isaac moved into university accommodation together. After a break, they worked on a new product range for Tees and Coffee between lectures and assessments. They bought an embroidery machine, a sewing machine and a heat press. Their student flat became an order hub and storage and distribution centre. They created social media content and T-shirts and hoodies with socially driven messages that quickly sold on their website. They took orders from university students and others in London and Cardiff.

Relationship with Student Communities

Pushpit and Isaac implemented social media campaigns not only to promote their products but also to spread social and ecological messages. Two young people were speaking to like-minded peers who were open to informative, motivating messages. They created an online campaign – Flush Fast Fashion – highlighting their sustainable streetwear, branded with meaningful messages.

Tees and Coffee T-shirts and hoodies displayed powerful sustainability quotes to inspire wearers to take social action, reduce waste and become sustainable, socially aware consumers.

Challenges

Tees and Coffee learnt the hard way about planning and contingency when an order from Cardiff University was much larger than Pushpit and Isaac had anticipated, and nearly 200 hoodies arrived late due to the continuing COVID-19 pandemic. When they did eventually arrive, they all needed to be embroidered with a logo and student initials. Hard work, determination and resilience enabled them to get the order out on time, and a second order was placed the following semester.

The Future

Pushpit has graduated and now works as an analyst at Elixir Management Consultants. Isaac is in his fourth year architecture studies. They recently decided it was time to close Tees and Coffee and move on, given the life opportunities coming their way.

> We envision our products to have a positive impact on our planet by controlling global climate change [while] simultaneously [not] hurting other people; if Tees and Coffee can help in this movement, our goal will be achieved. Pushpit Bhardwaj

Congratulations to these two young entrepreneurs who have indeed achieved their goals.

Forest Green Rovers

Anthony Samuel and Carolyn Strong

> Forest Green Rovers is dedicated to becoming a truly sustainable football club, a world first. We aim to make it a place where we can demonstrate eco-thinking and technology to a new audience, football fans. Indeed, we believe that we have the opportunity to introduce sustainability to the wider world of sport, not just football. (Forest Green Rovers Footprint Report, 2019)

Synopsis

Forest Green Rovers Football Club was established in 1889 (Barnard, 2006). One hundred and twenty-eight years later, in 2017, the club turned professional following its promotion to Division Two in the English Football League.

Recently mainstream, online and social media have taken an interest in Forest Green Rovers who implement triple bottom line sustainability practices (Elkington, 1994) in strategic operations of the professional football club. These strategies have attracted new supporters and mainstream media interest, with the BBC and national British newspapers, including the *Guardian* and *The Times* reporting on the football club's unique sustainable green practices.

> Caulkin (2017) ran the headline in The Times *'Forest Green Rovers – the club where meat is off the menu, and the pitch is fed seaweed'*. While Forbes (2020) ran with an article titled *'A wooden Stadium, Organic Pitch and vegan Pies: Welcome to the Worlds Greenest Soccer Club.'*

History of Forest Green Rovers

Established in 1889, Forest Green Rovers is a community-led football club located in the town of Nailsworth in Gloucestershire, England. The club works closely with the local community, having established a charity to educate and motivate people through football.

In 2010, Dale Vince, the founder of the Gloucestershire-based energy company Ecotricity[1] became a major shareholder of Forest Green Rovers and was appointed club chairman. In 2011, the club became the first and 100% vegan, carbon-neutral sustainable football. Key to Forest Green Rovers' success has been the vision of Dale Vince to take the sustainability message to a new audience and thus contribute to 'long-term behavioural change, within the club of course, but also from our supporters and the rest of the sporting world' (Forest Green Rovers Sustainability Report, 2019).

---

1 https://www.ecotricity.co.uk/

https://doi.org/10.1515/9783110756142-015

Dale Vince is not a traditional energy industry multi-millionaire, He has a maverick past (as a New Age traveller) and green visions of the future (a vegan Britain entirely self-sufficient in green gas). He has an interest in many sustainable enterprises, from rainforest regeneration to electric vehicles, documentaries like Seaspiracy[2] to tidal lagoons, Carbon neutral diamonds to green football (Goodwin, 2022).

Small Business Enterprise

A Sustainable British Football Club?

Forest Green Rovers' has a holistic operational approach to running the club as a sustainable an innovative expansion of traditional approaches to corporate social responsibility. These practices are evident for all to witness, from their organic and vegan football pitch vegetable to solar panel floodlights, recycled water systems, underground heat sources, electric vehicle charging points, solar-powered robot mowers, and eco-meadow and eco walking trail to the more novel practices of only serving vegan food to management, players and supporters (Forest Green Rovers Sustainability Report, 2019).

This commitment is evidenced through the club's achievement of accreditation from Eco-Management and Audit Schemes in 2017; the offsetting of carbon football matchday tickets: kit manufacturing with a local UK manufacturer who utilise bamboo fibre and coffee waste in their manufacturing processes. Forest Green Rovers have achieved a number of sustainable benchmarks, including:
–   16% reduction in their carbon emissions
–   44% reduction of individual spectator's carbon footprint
–   40% reduction in energy use
–   57% reduction in water consumption.

Having measured the club's carbon footprint since 2011, adopting a carbon-neutral gas tariff in 2021, they have made significant improvements to reduce the football club's carbon footprint reducing it by 53% in 10 years (Forest Green Rovers Climate Study, 2021). Table 1 offers an indication of how this was achieved.

Promotion Innovations

Forest Green Rovers have found a place of interest in the world football community with no promotional effort. Interest in a sustainable football club has gained momen-

---

2 https://www.theguardian.com/commentisfree/2021/apr/07/seaspiracy-earth-oceans-destruction-industrial-fishing

Table 1: Forest Green Rovers emissions and carbon footprint detailed in the club's Climate Study 2021.

Consumption	2018/19 Emissions (tonnes)	2019/20 Emissions (tonnes)
Electricity	0	0
Gas	36.8	1.98
Water	2.9	6.6
Transport pool vehicles	10.2	8.65
Transport coach	33.9	18.25
TOTAL	**83.8**	**35.46**

tum in the UK and worldwide. FIFA, the world football governing body, have identified Forest Green Rovers as *'the world's greenest football club'* (BBC, 2018). In 2018, the United Nations certified Forest Green Rovers as *'the world's first carbon-neutral football club'* while also appointing Chairman Dale Vince as a UN Climate ambassador (McLaughlin, 2018). *The Financial Times* reported on the success of Forest Green Rovers' sustainability initiatives, commenting on the fact that sustainability is *'big winner'* that has put the club in a unique and competitive position in football (Murad, 2019) – in 2019, the club reported a 19% higher turnover than any other professional football club operating at the same divisional level (Murad, 2019). Such media interest and reporting have promoted and reaffirmed Forest Green Rovers' authentic and unique commitment to a strategic green approach and sustainable operational practices in management of a professional football club. This lead to the support, respect and interest of the general public, footballing governing bodies, eco-conscious values organisation, third-party certifying organisations, other sporting organisations and the wider football supporting community (Samuel, 2022).

Relationships with the Community

Forest Green Rovers' green and sustainable approach to football has impacted on the changing landscape of the club's supporters, the social impact of the vegan/organic playing surface, and the provision of vegan food in its catering outlets.

Forest Rovers Supporters

Forest Green Rovers' commitment to sustainability has established a new supporter community located in 20 countries outside of the UK, including Russia, Norway and Holland. In 2019, the launch of the bamboo supporters kit sold out within 24 hours across 16 different countries, including Australia, South Korea and Malaysia (Forest

Green Rovers Footprint Report, 2019). The growth in football supporters' interest is evident in the significant media attention the club received – for example the club reported the following in media coverage in 2019:

- 2,303 media articles published in international publications
- 37,442 Facebook *'likes'* in 2018
- 27,657 current Twitter followers who describe Forest Green Rovers as a respectful, open and family-friendly football club.

Forest Green Rovers are very strong on our family values. The club has a commitment to ensuring a safe environment which is established with the input of Forest Green Rovers Young Ambassadors' program which brings local children's voices to the club management; for example they provide dedicated spaces in match day programmes and on the club website to host Young Ambassador blogs.

At the start of every season, the club gifts 500 football kits to local children and gives them free entry to many matches. The club has strong links with local schools through player and staff visits, sustainable education days and vegan cooking sessions held at the clubhouse. Forest Green Rovers' links with local schools and its proactive community engagement have developed a social foundation that has helped the club become known as a *'friendly respectful club.'*

The Football Pitch Playing Surface

In 2021, Forest Green Rovers constructed an organic and vegan playing surface which is maintained with ethically sourced seaweed, sugars, coconut, sand and bacteria. Forest Green Rovers' drive to share its sustainability knowledge and expertise about the green pitch playing surface has resulted in the club hosting the leaders of several world-renowned sporting institutions keen to learn more about the management of sustainable organic playing surfaces – including Wembley Arena, Wimbledon Tennis Club, Real Bettis Football Club and Aston Villa (Samuel, 2022).

Vegan Catering Outlets

Significant praise and criticism have been attributed to Forest Green Rovers' vegan-only food policy. The exclusively vegan offer has in the main been positively received and it is now understood that most Forest Green Rovers stakeholders are happy to consume vegan food on match day.

Forest Green Rovers (Source: Anthony Samuel).

The Future

Forest Green Rovers' pursuit of a green and sustainable football club has a future focus on the construction of football stadium. The club is seeking the construction of a ecologically football stadium. They have been granted planning permission to build

the world's first all-wooden 5,000 capacity *'Eco Park'* stadium, which has been described as: *'the greenest football stadium in the world'* (McLaughlin, 2018).

References

Barnard, T. (2006). *Something to shout about: The history of Forest Green Rovers FC*. The History Press.

BBC. (2018). https://www.bbc.co.uk/news/uk-england-gloucestershire-45677536

Caulkin, G. (2017). Forest Green Rovers: The club were meat is off the menu and the pitch is fed seaweed. https://www.thetimes.co.uk/article/forest-green-rovers-theclub-where-meat-is-off-the-menu-and-the-pitch-is-fed-seaweed-kp2zkw35d

Elkington, J. (1994). Towards the sustainable corporation: Win-win-win business strategies for sustainable development. *California Management Review, 36*(2), 90–100.

Forest Green Rovers Climate Study. (2021). https://assets.ctfassets.net/f42pa1j7pq2p/12OE6paUx AtFptwQjxG6sC/6966c4cb1471cb78cc69420d9aaebf60/FGR-UN-Doc-2021.pdf

Forest Green Rovers Footprint Report. (2019). Forest Green Rovers to compensate carbon emissions related to fan travel. https://sustainabilityreport.com/2019/07/31/forestgreen-rovers

Goodwin, R. (2022). 'I don't try and fit in': energy boss Dale Vince on Fracking, Farage and going Green. https://www.theguardian.com/business/2022/nov/20/energy-boss-dale-vince-fracking-farage-and-going-green

Kidd, R. (2020). A wooden stadium, organic pitch, and vegan pies: welcome to the "worlds greenest" soccer club. https://www.forbes.com/sites/robertkidd/2020/02/17/a-wooden-stadium-organic-pitch-and-vegan-pies-welcome-to-the-worlds-greenest-soccer-club/?sh=229b197a14b2

McLaughlin, L. (2018). Forest Green Rovers granted planning permission for all wooden stadium. https://www.theguardian.com/football/2019/dec/29/forest-green-rovers-granted-planning-permission-for-all-wooden-stadium

Murad, A. (2019). Green credentials prove big winner for tiny English football team. https://www.ft.com/content/d66ba036-763a-11e9-be7d-6d846537acab

Samuel, A. (2022). Detalie de caso: Como un club incorpora lo Social y ambiental a sue nucleo de negocio. In *Manuel del metodo fair Play Social* (pp. 76–81). Editado Fundacion LaiLiga Enero 2022.

The Pembrokeshire Beach Food Company

Our aim at Cafe Môr – The Pembrokeshire Beach Food Company is simply: to create imaginative, innovative and delicious food; to share our passions for food, sea, beach and life; to inspire sustainable business and promote conservation; to celebrate our seas and beaches, offering fresh seafood supplies and foraged wild ingredients, with our online shop, to help you create exciting dishes of the highest quality. Jonathan Williams[1]

Synopsis

The Pembrokeshire Beach Food Company was founded by Jonathan Williams, a self-confessed seaweed fanatic and dreamer who returned to the Pembrokeshire coast after a successful management career in the city. His business life is complicated, consisting of a beach restaurant, a public house, an online, seaweed-based food outlet and a rum brand. Jonathan has earned the title Pioneer King of Seaweed among his local, tourist and online customers.[2]

The Pembrokeshire Beach Food Company is a small business for which the core ingredient is seaweed foraged off the coast of West Wales. It produces seaweed products, mainly laverbread, seasonings and condiments, as well as a range of dried and frozen seaweed. The company also runs a first-of-its-kind, mobile, solar-powered seaweed kitchen – Cafe Môr.

Cafe Môr began in an iconic, former seaweed boat, The Josie June,[3] which, from 2012, parked in the car park of Freshwater West on the coast of Pembrokeshire, West Wales, between March and October each year, selling laver-seaweed-based burgers, crab and lobster sandwiches and seaweed brownies to surfers and holidaymakers. The Josie June is now anchored at the Old Point House,[4] a historic restaurant, a few minutes' drive from Freshwater West. The new location on the coastal path has an outside beach bar, a garden, seating overlooking the bay and steps down to the beach.

---

1 Visit Pembrokeshire website: https://www.visitpembrokeshire.com
2 https://www.walesonline.co.uk/whats-on/food-drink-news/man-behind-beachside-cafe-pub-27201813
3 https://beachfood.co.uk/blogs/captains-blog/notes-from-the-unsuccessful-money-man-example-3-the-boat
4 https://www.theoldpointhouse.wales/

https://doi.org/10.1515/9783110756142-016

Jonathan Williams with a seaweed pile (Source: Jonathan Williams).

History

Jonathan started Cafe Môr in 2011 after realising that returning to his coastal home and all it had to offer – including fresh seafood – could provide him with an exciting business prospect. This realisation caused him to move from Swindon, quitting his business career as a sustainability adviser, to Pembrokeshire to open a seafood stall. At his first stall – set up at a local farm shop one summer – Jonathan spent fourteen hours a day preparing and cooking a variety of products, including Pembrokeshire sushi, salads, quiches, deli products and crab and lobster.

The seafood stall led to the restoration of the Josie June, allowing Jonathan to tour around the area and attend festivals and events. The first 5 years of The Pembrokeshire Beach Food Company involved towing The Josie June to farmers' markets and music festivals, including Glastonbury. The company was awarded the British Street Food Award for Best Street Food Seller, and just 2 weeks before his daughter was born, Jonathan was providing seaweed-based food to athletes at the London 2012 Olympic Athletes Village.[5]

After an incredibly stressful 5 years, Jonathan, now with a young family, decided to anchor The Josie June at Freshwater West car park, selling seaweed-based burgers to surfers from sunrise to dusk. Cafe Môr relocated to the Old Point House in 2022.

---

5 https://www.bbc.com/news/uk-wales-65200431

As well as running the beach-food outlet, Jonathan and his team market a range of fresh and dried seaweed-based seasonings, butters and snack products, and seaweed-infused drinks, including the popular, seaweed-spiced Barti Rum.

Themes

Beyond developing a seaweed food and drink culture, there are economic and environmental impacts of harvesting seaweed for production. Jonathan harvests wild seaweed around the perimeter of the Pembrokeshire coast – it is legal for anyone to harvest seaweed on the coastline as long as it is floating and unattached. Seaweed can be harvested sustainably but harvesting must consider the seaweed habitat and its role as a natural coastal-defence line.

Seaweed is high in nutrients, containing many oxidants, vitamins A, C and E, iron and protein. It has been used for traditional food products throughout Welsh history:

> Laverbread is rooted in Welsh history as a vital source of nutrition. This high-energy food source was particularly crucial for hardworking pit workers in the South Wales mining valleys where it became a staple breakfast food. (Turner, 2023)

Small Business Enterprise

An alternative life and location for The Josie June became the next stage in The Pembrokeshire Beach Food Company's journey. The company set itself up in the car park at Freshwater West, where the outdoor seaweed cafe depended on the weather and changing surfing conditions. The business was booming in the spring and summer, but outside peak surfing season, revenues were low, and employees were not required.

Jonathan needed to source an annual income to support his young family and to help the local, seasonal workforce during the winter months. The Pembrokeshire Beach Food Company developed a seaweed shop and distribution chain, supplying 250 outlets with seaweed ketchup, sea herbs, seaweed pesto and other ingredients used in Cafe Môr products. Tourists who had bought products at the cafe were now able to purchase them online when they returned home.

In a move to increase revenue, the company successfully launched Barti Rum – a Caribbean rum infused with Pembrokeshire laver seaweed and inspired by Barti Ddu ('Black Bart'), a Pembrokeshire-born pirate whose story had fascinated Jonathan.[6]

---

6 https://www.worldhistory.org/Bartholomew_Roberts/

Pembrokeshire Beachfood Good Food Award 2023/24 (Source: Jonathan Williams).

Pembrokeshire Beachfood seaweed food products (Source: Jonathan Williams).

The Online Seaweed Food Range

As products seasoned with seaweed handpicked from the Welsh coast became popular among Jonathan's customers, tourists started to request seasoning and sauces for home cooking. The popular Seaweed Ketchup Sauce (Kelpchup), loved by surfers at Freshwater West and the winner of a Great Taste Award in 2022, can now be bought at the cafe or from the online shop, along with a range of other seaweed products and gifts.

Barti Rum

Jonathan aimed to produce and market the best-tasting spiced rum possible; the product specification was that he would want to drink it himself. Jonathan created a bold rum infused with Pembrokeshire foraged seaweed. Barti Spiced Rum's marketing proposition is positivity and passion that celebrates the Welsh coast.

The Barti Rum brand is prioritising sustainability and innovation and aiming to become carbon neutral – a huge challenge given the distilling of the rum, the production of the glass bottle, the bottle stopper and the label and the transportation of the product. Jonathan and his team are planting seaweed in strategic locations off the coast of Pembrokeshire in an effort to offset Barti Rum's carbon emissions. They are also researching and developing other initiatives to ensure carbon neutrality.

The Future

Barti Rum is currently working towards becoming a certified B Corp brand,[7] which means the brand promises to always make environmentally sustainable decisions that contribute positively to society.

Jonathan's creativity and passion are never-ending. He is currently working with a team of marine biologists on a project off the coast of Milford Haven, West Wales, where they are monitoring the habitat and emissions of kelp ropes to research the viability of seaweed as a carbon capture mechanism. Jonathan shares his passion for using seaweed as a carbon capture tool in an online blog[8] where he discusses his plans to learn about how he and others can use seaweed to offset carbon and his plans to commercially farm seaweed. Research confirms his belief that seaweed can be used to mitigate climate change. For example, Ross et al. (2023) have found that commercial seaweed farming can protect and restore wild seaweed forests and expand sustainable, close-to-shore seaweed growth, which can lead to the offsetting of industrial carbon di-

7 https://bcorporation.uk/
8 https://www.bartirum.wales/barti-and-the-big-blue

oxide emissions; they have also found that sinking seaweed in deep sea leads to the sequestration[9] of carbon dioxide.

Research by Strong-Wright and Taylor (2022) aims to quantify the carbon offsetting potential of our seas, including how seaweed forests can be enhanced to restore high levels of carbon; the research also aims to gain an understanding of how seaweed can contribute to the ocean carbon cycle.[10] The Pembrokeshire Beach Food Company is sponsoring similar academic research at Swansea University, which is modelling the use of seaweed in the Atlantic Ocean off the coast of West Wales.

Few entrepreneurs have taken their passion for the sea to the level of creating a community-led food and drink business: a small, local business enterprise that not only strives to use local ingredients and reduce its carbon footprint but also provides long-term local training and employment based on the Jonathon's moral compass and business philosophy of love Food, love Beach, love Sea, love life.

References

Ross, F. W. R., Boyd, P. W., Filbee-Dexter, K., Watanabe, K., Ortega, A., Krause-Jensen, D., Lovelock, C., Sondak, C. F. A., Bach, L. T., Duarte, C. M., Serrano, O., Beardall, J., Tarbuck, P., & Macreadie, P. I. (2023). Potential role of seaweeds in climate change mitigation. *Science of the Total Environment, 885*, 163699.
Strong-Wright, J., & Taylor, J. R. (2022). Modeling the growth potential of the kelp *Saccharina Latissima* in the North Atlantic. *Sec. Ocean Solutions, 8.* https://doi.org/10.3389/fmars.2021.793977
Turner, R. (2023). Welsh Laverbread. https://businesswales.gov.wales/foodanddrink/how-we-can-help/new-uk-geographical-indication-gi-schemes-0/welsh-laverbread-pdo

---

9 Sequestration is a process which captures and stores atmospheric carbon dioxide in the natural environment.

10 https://www.frontiersin.org/articles/10.3389/fmars.2021.793977/full

Part Three: **Small Family Businesses**

Let Them See Cake celebration cake (Source: Ryan Rowe; photo: Marie Francesca).

https://doi.org/10.1515/9783110756142-017

Melin Tregwynt workshop (Source: Amanda Griffith).

The following six case studies are all small family businesses with very different beginnings and approaches to their business strategies.

The Gower Gin Company is a small, sustainable and environmentally friendly distillery in the Gower in West Wales. Founded and run by a husband and wife team producing gins created using botanicals foraged in the Gower.

Água Na Boca, Boia Bar and Restaurante Olhos N'Agua are a collection of family-owned restaurants based in the Algarve in Portugal. Founded, expanded and managed by a family team of restaurateurs.

Let Them See Cake creates hand-crafted buttercream cakes for any occasion alongside running a homely café offering a range of cakes and brunch.

Big Moose Coffee Co is an award-winning coffee shop working towards the prevention of homelessness and supporting mental health issues.

Melin Tregwynt is a traditional mill run by the Griffiths family for over 100 years. It was owned and managed by Eifion and Amanda Griffiths until 2022, when it became an Employee Owned Trust.

Antagrade Electrical was established in 1983 by a group of friends, and it later became a family-run business. It specializes in railway traction power and infrastructure.

The Gower/Gŵyr Gin Company

A micro distillery is in a converted bike shed in the village of Port Eynon on Gower. We have an absolute passion for gin and are constantly developing new recipes based on the botanicals found on Gower. They aim is to make small batch craft gin which encapsulates the freshness of the sea and the aromas of the coast and dunes that surround us. https://www.thegowergincompany.wales

Synopsis

Andrew and Siân Brookes are the husband and wife founders and directors of the Gower Gin Company (Gŵyr in Welsh). They began producing gin in a bike shed at their coastal Welsh home in 2017.

Andrew studied geography with botany and has always had an interest in flora and wild edible plants. He had a long and successful career as a Management Consultant before retiring early to spend more time with his family in West Wales. He is the joint director, distiller, responsible sales and finance director and the inspirational creator of pioneering gins at Gower Gin.

Siân studied French and Spanish, until recently she was a language lecturer at Swansea University. She is the joint director, business strategist, marketing director and creator of web design at Gower Gin.

As a small family enterprise, they must take responsibility for aspects of the business for a small gin brand; this comprises – recipe building and product design, including the bottle, the logo, the label and the packaging for online orders. Andrew runs the production of gin while Siân works on sales and marketing, web design and supplier contacts, including sourcing ingredients and packaging. Andrew takes responsibility for the finances, and Siân develops and maintains good relationships with business contacts. Both directors spend a great amount of time at Gin Festivals, planning and hosting Gin tastings and creating cocktails to post about on social media. During COVID, these events became virtual, with customers sending gin and instructions in the post while Andrew and Siân hosted from their garden. A huge variety of tasks make running a small family business exciting.

https://doi.org/10.1515/9783110756142-018

Andrew and Siân Brookes (Source: Siân Brookes; photo: Teahouse photography).

History

As a birthday present, Andrew took Siân to a gin festival in Portello Road where you could make your own gin and learn about the history of gin and its intracity. As the day progressed, Andrew and Siân began to think that *we could do this.* They came up with the idea to create a gin based on the area where they lived – the Gower Peninsula in coastal rural West Wales, an area of outstanding natural beauty. Almost every business in the area has Gower in its title, a powerful brand name with deep meaning and a wide knowledge based on its tourism.

Their concept is to make gins based on the flavours of Gower's locally foraged botanicals. Their first gin Gŵyr is flavoured with wild bronze and green fennel which grows on the coast wild, fresh zest of lemon and grapefruit. They decided to launch in 2017 with a post on Facebook in partnership with a wine and spirits merchant. Within 4 days, they had 28,000 likes – a direct illustration of the level of interest in a Welsh gin.

One of the keys to the success of Gower Gin is that they were the first gin to launch in West Wales and the fifth in Wales, gaining first mover advantage in the market.

Siân created the distinctive blue and white stripe label (and subsequent branding) based on their love of Brittiany; the stripes indicate the sea they love and connect their lives in France and in Wales. Their Welsh identity is a factor in the gin's success, and customers were asked if they preferred Gower or the Welsh translation Gŵyr; research found that they preferred the Welsh version even with those who did not speak Welsh.

Small Business Enterprise

Eighteen months after the launch, Siân and Andrew went to the Junipalooza Gin Festival[1] in London, the most prestigious and the biggest show in the country. Their stand was beside Whitley Neill Gin[2] on one side and Sacred Gin[3] on the other, both very strong brands that invested heavily in their stands and have high-profile sales teams. Andrew and Siân had a low-cost marketing tool, Gower Gin Fudge which attracted many happy visitors to their stand and generated interest in the festival and online.

Siân observed how the big brands created customer interest and loyalty. They gave away branded merchandise, including glasses, stickers and rewards. The next show they went to, they took stickers, such a simple marketing tool that resulted in adults waiting patiently in line for a sticker – this led to the realisation that it is *little things* that can market a small business and generate customer loyalty.

Developing the Brand

Gower started with one gin product with no intention of adding any other. However, they quickly realised they needed to keep people interested, so they decided they would develop a new gin every year; each one has a story and is created with a Welsh theme in mind. Each new gin keeps the stripe theme, and Siân adapts it to fit the story of the new product keeping a cohesive identity across the range.

Gower has built a customer community with gin tastings at the distillery,[4] attendance at gin festivals and online relationships with their growing consumer population.

A core and in-depth understanding of the consumer and the market is key to Gower Gin's success. The gin demographic is increasingly getting younger, and this consumer group has a taste for a sweet and fruity gin; gin is no longer a niche older persons drink formally known as 'Mother Ruin' from the eighteenth century – it is

---

1 https://www.spiritssociety.com/junipalooza-london
2 https://whitleyneill.com/
3 https://sacredgin.com/
4 https://www.thegowergincompany.wales/visit-us/

now a trendy gin cocktail fun and young drink. To accommodate the consumer segments, Gower has the dual strategy of creating a core dry gin and an evolving range of sweet and fruit gins. They also have two market segments: the end consumer and organisations looking to outsource the creation and distilling of their own gin brand.

Gower also provides a range of large contracts and bespoke gin for hotels and festivals. These customers visit the distillery to formulate and make their gin. This reduces the cost of personalised branded gins to the end consumer as they utilise Gower's distillery and their licensing rights – this is a lucrative marketing for the small business providing a guaranteed income; they currently make over 80 gins for other companies. The outcome of this is that Andrew and Siân have the freedom to do exactly what they like with their own range and the freedom to take risks with their innovation and creativity while having a steady income to support the business.

The power of connections is essential to small business enterprises. Andrew strongly feels that the power of partnership and connection launched to Gower/Gŵyr locally. All marketing and promotions are developed and implemented in-house by Siân who has an inherent understanding of the extensive customer data generated from sales and online interactions.

Siân has successfully made the brand visible. It is easy to identify, easy to spot at events and it has a consistent and engaging image across social media. The stripes run through all marketing campaigns and have generated a huge amount of interest and online traffic – with customers posting their own stripe-based gin photos.

Gower Gin's distinctive stripe branding (Source: Siân Brookes; photo: Teahouse photography).

Gŵyr Rhosili (Source: Siân Brookes; photo: Teahouse photography).

Sustainability

Gower strives to achieve sustainability through their ingredients sources, production (they are powered by 100% green electricity), packaging, energy, supply chain and social responsibility. They have a no-plastic policy, for example the bottle caps are cellulose; mail order packing is sustainable[5] gin can be purchased (at a lower price) in an eco-friendly refill pouch which can be sent back to Port Eynon to be recycled.

Andrew and Siân strive to be sustainable but recognise that they could do better – all small businesses can be more sustainable, but this takes innovation, resources and ultimately financial investment and costs to the consumer.

The Community

Andrew and Siân's community support is core to their family business; based in a rural coastal village, they support other small businesses and commission merchandise from local craft markers, including gin pins, aprons and ceramic branded hearts. This merchandise does not make money but gets people engaged in the brand and makes it distinctive among the gin crowd – while supporting local craft makers.

The community focus and support provided by Gower Gin are quietly evident in their production and distribution of hand sanitiser during COVID-19. As soon as it was legally possible, Andrew and Siân started to produce *Glân* hand sanitiser following the World Health Organization-approved recipe. In spring 2020, they became one of the first gin distilleries to convert production for the duration of COVID-19 restrictions.

At the start of the crisis, they were inundated with requests for hand sanitiser as the national media suggested alcohol manufacturers could produce approved products. Within a few weeks Gower Gin produced sanitiser to support ambulance crews, hospitals, schools, police, nurses, midwives, social care centres, doctor's surgeries, care homes and palliative care centres across West Wales.

The Future

Andrew and Siân have sustainable and community business principle convictions. As a successful family business, they focus on the environment and the sustainability of the brand despite the financial investment and ultimate premium price to the end consumer. Andrew strongly believes that to succeed in a competitive market as a small family business, one must focus *on your own game and what you can control*. They are an inspiration to future rural family business entrepreneurs with the advice – *follow your convictions.*

---

5 https://www.flexi-hex.com/

Água Na Boca, Boia Bar and Restaurante Olhos N'Agua

Synopsis

The Castela family are part of Salema's history; generations of Castelas are at the heart of this fishing village in the Vicentine Coast Natural Park, which is one of the smallest popular tourist destinations in Europe. A charming working fishing village, a wide stretch of sand on the windswept Atlantic littered with a mix of small fishing boats on the sand tethered beside sunbeds and families enjoying a beach vacation. In the peak holiday season, the sand is populated by fishermen attending to their nets, sun seekers, children building sandcastles and playing the sea, world champion kite surfers, surfers and bodyboarders (Knight, 2018).

As a family they closely work together running three popular restaurants (among other small businesses including holiday accommodation) in the village. Água Na Boca restaurant and Garrafeira, Boia Bar and Olhos N'Agua are Mediterranean, local Portuguese cuisine restaurants; they are all owned and managed by Paulo Castela, his wife Irene and their children.

During peak season, March to October, Paulo works 18-hour days. He credits his wife, Irene, of over 30 years for the creativity, drive and passion behind the family business. Paulo is clearly a family man, which is evident when observing how much he adores his infant granddaughter.

https://doi.org/10.1515/9783110756142-019

Boia Bar Branding (Source: Carolyn Strong).

The History

The opening of Faro Airport in 1965 began the tourist invasion of the Algarve, developing the area from a region of sleepy fishing towns into a vibrant and cosmopolitan tourist destination. Investment in the local infrastructure and roads connecting the Algarve to Lisbon and Spain in the 1990s further developed tourism with British, German, French and Dutch, and other Europeans, and global travellers, seeking sun, relaxation and good food holidays (Algarve Retreats, 2023).

Fishing formed a core part of life in the Algarve, while fishing is still prominent in the community, it is not as valuable to the local economy as tourism: fishing boats were drawn up by teams of men and women who waited on the beach for the boats to come to shore, these have given way to tractors (Livermore, 2017) which now form one of the attractions attracting tourists to coastal towns and villages. The Algarve has retained its fishing trade and values and the cobbled streets are lined with whitewashed fishermen's cottages. Wooden boats catch sea bass, bream, octopus, sardines and oysters; tourists watch the fishing boats towed from the sea by tractors and fishermen unloading their catch and then mending their nets each day from the restaurants overlooking the Atlantic Ocean (Simply Salema, 2023). The passion for food in the Algarve dates back to the Roman and Arabic presence in the area; ingredients and recipes reflect the catch from the sea and the produce of the land (Clube Vinho Portuguese, 2023).

Paulo's family heritage is embedded in the Algarve, born in the village, and raised in a fishing family, his heart and spirit are deeply rooted in the local community which he supports by providing training and employment in the restaurants, sourcing of local produce and ingredients and continuous work for local trades people.

When Paulo was a young teenager, his father became seriously unwell. As an indication of the hardship in the village at the time, Mr Castela senior had to walk to a local market to purchase a pair of shoes to go to a hospital appointment in the nearby city. Sadly Paulo's father passed away, leaving him as the young head of the family responsible for supporting and caring for his mother and others. He left school to work in the local restaurants, where he became a skilled busser, runner, waiter, bartender, front-of-house host and restaurant manager. He fulfilled his aspiration to own a restaurant, opening *Água Na Boca* with his wife Irene and later taking over *Boia Bar* where he worked for many years. A third restaurant followed when they concerted a beachside building into *Olhos N'Agua*. Paulo credits his wife Irene for the success of the restaurants, her culinary expertise, creativity, interior design expertise, and her determination and devotion to their family. Their strength of mind in providing for their family is witnessed over the summer period when they work up to 18 hours a day, 7 days a week during the peak tourist season – over half of the calendar year they have no rest, the encounter new challenges every day from missing ingredients to power cuts and weather storms, they work as a family to deliver a quality dining experience to a wide range of clientele.

Small Business Enterprise in the Algarve

Paulo and Irene own and manage three successful restaurants, each having a unique offering in terms of location, ambience and menu, while there is a common thread of attention to detail, quality of food and customer service. All three restaurants are efficiently run by trained staff, offer beautiful table settings in spaces expertly designed to fit the coastal location and tourist environment and provide expertly prepared local food.

While the location of a coastal restaurant is key to its popularity, the quality of the food and service is essential to its long-term success. The eating experience must match and indeed exceed expectations for customers to make recommendations and return to book a table in the future. Paulo prides himself on his attention to detail and the superior dining experience provided in all three restaurants (and in the Água Na Boca Garrafeira[1]), there are no shortcuts – every aspect of the dining experience has been styled from the interior design to the silverware. Each space has a beautiful interior, stylish furniture, ambient music and trained staff who pay full attention to every customer's needs.

Boia Bar table setting (Source: Carolyn Strong).

---

1 A Garrafeira is a Portuguese wine cellar were wine is preserved and served under special conservation conditions.

Boia Bar restaurant view (Source: Carolyn Strong).

Água Na Boca, Boia Bar and Olhos N'Agua have beautiful interiors style by Irene and perfected with consideration of every aspect of the dining experience. Research by Mariani (2021) considers what makes a good restaurant, asserting that restaurant perfection is achievable through the efforts and dedication of the owners – Paulo and Irene's attention to the design and fabric of the décor, the quality and design of the silverware, glassware and table linen is flawless. The table accessories reflect the individual style and elegance of each of the three restaurants and the menus – the glassware is elegant, the silverware stylish and the high-quality table linen matches the colour scheme. There is research psychology to support the role that music plays in creating the ambience of a restaurant. Studies have found a 9.1% difference in sales when playing music that matches an ambience of the restaurant in comparison to playing popular, well-liked tunes (Absoluteci, 2023); Água Na Boca, Boia Bar and Olhos N'Agua's music playlists contribute to the atmosphere, mood and dining experiences of each restaurant throughout the day.

All ingredients are sourced locally from suppliers who are family, friends and collaborators in the community. Fresh produce is delivered daily; suppliers deliver once to cover the needs of all three restaurants. This guarantees quality and a rigid control over the logistics of procurement, delivery and storage.

The quality of the restaurant experience is dependent on the skills and expertise of staff; Irene and Marcelo (their son) are accomplished, trained, proficient chefs who are experts in sourcing quality ingredients, menu development, stunning plating and presentation of food. Paulo has a skilled approach to table management developed over many years of experience. This skill maximises table turnover, reduces waiting times and manages customer expectations. Teamwork is evident across this family-owned business, from ordering ingredients to managing three restaurants effectively and efficiently, particularly during the peak summer season when all three restaurants are full to capability from the time of early morning opening to late night closing.

Água Na Boca

Água Na Boca is smart and sophisticated. Situated on the cobbled street a short walk to the beach this is upmarket establishment has a reputation for being amongst the finest eateries in the Algarve. Owner Paulo takes pride in serving a range of meat, fish, local and international dishes, with a wide selection of wines. https://simplysalema.com/salema/restaurants-in-salema

Água Na Boca is the fine dining[2] experience in the family restaurant collection. It offers a creative discerning menu, excellent service and the ambience of a superior dining experience with attention to detail and the consideration of every aspect of the fine dining experience – a more formal and elegant restaurant experience than that offered at the relaxed Boia Bar.

Boia Bar

A simple but well-run and popular beachfront restaurant overlooking the Atlantic ocean has a friendly welcome. Serving a variety of fresh grilled fish and meats, and Caldeirada de Peixe[3]. Boia bar has stunning seaside views. https://simplysalema.com/salema/restaurants-in-salema

Boia Bar is the long-established beachside restaurant where Paulo was employed as a teenager, allowing him to financially support his mother and family. The restaurant is located on the beach promenade and offers views of the Atlantic Ocean from every

---

2 The Cambridge University dictionary defines fine dining as '*a style of eating that usually takes place in expensive restaurants, where especially good food is served to people, often in a formal way*'.
3 A traditional Portuguese fish stew of a range of locally available fish and potatoes.

table. The menu offers locally sourced seafood, Portuguese meat and fish. The location of this restaurant is magnificent, a few paces from the Atlantic Ocean with breathtaking beach views and beautifully designed interior offering a family-friendly welcome from skilled service staff. The simple attention to detail, including table linen, silverware and glassware complement the high-quality food and service offering to ensure customers have a unique, satisfying outdoor experience.

Olhos N'Agua

> Located on the seafront overlooking the Atlantic with stunning views and a relaxed ambiance. A clean and contemporary setting, serving fresh fish, seafood, meat, pasta, and tapas. Less formal and more relaxed than its sister restaurant Água Na Boca. https://simplysalema.com/salema/restaurants-in-salema

Olhos N'Agua is a beach bar and restaurant with a relaxed setting, a few paces from the beach with views of the sand and the ocean. Diners enjoy local fish and seafood, or afternoon drinks served by friendly staff to the background sound of relaxing music in calming minimalist restaurant décor.

The Future

Paulo and Irene Castela continue to successfully manage the family restaurant business. They provide local training and employment, source ingredients from local suppliers and generate local economic revenue for the village. They have long-lasting good customer relationships; they do not need to invest in advertising or marketing as word-of-mouth communications for all three establishments is generated by their loyal, satisfied customers. The family business is extending with the support of the next generation of Castela entrepreneurs.

References

Absoluteci. (2023). https://www.absoluteci.co.uk/blog/5-restaurant-features-that-shape-a-good-ambience
Algarve Retreats. (2023). https://www.algarve-retreats.com
Clube Vinho Portugueses. (2023). https://www.clubevinhosportugueses.pt/turismo/historia-e-origem-da-carne-de-porco-a-alentejana/
Knight, J. (2018). https://www.thetimes.co.uk/article/welcome-to-salema-in-the-secret-algarve
Livermore, H. (2017). Portugal: A Traveller's History. Cambridge University Press, 2017.
Mariani, J. (2021). What makes a perfect restaurant? Forbes 2nd September
Simply Salema. (2023). https://simplysalema.com/salema

Let Them See Cake

Carolyn Strong and Robert Bowen

Synopsis

Let Them See Cake is a celebration cake business and café based in Victoria Park in Cardiff, Wales. The business was created in July 2020 by entrepreneurs Gareth Davies and Ryan Rowe at the height of the COVID-19 pandemic. The business gained notoriety across the UK as part of a BBC docuseries on the business called 'Hot Cakes,' which followed the development of the business, describing it as 'Wales' most Instagramable cake shop.' Originally from Aberystwyth, Gareth Davies has been designing and producing cakes for many years, and prior to the COVID-19 pandemic, he produced various elaborate celebration cakes, entered cake decorating competitions and ran a business in teaching workshops cake decorating and sugar work. As this business activity was forced to stop during the COVID-19 lockdowns, Gareth, along with his partner Ryan, set up Let Them See Cake to provide mail order and delivery services of cake boxes. The success of this led to the opening of their café in Victoria Park in Cardiff, where the business has since grown by expanding its seating area in the café and offering brunch services. As of 2023, the business employs ten workers in the café and the business' industrial kitchen where the cakes are produced.

https://doi.org/10.1515/9783110756142-020

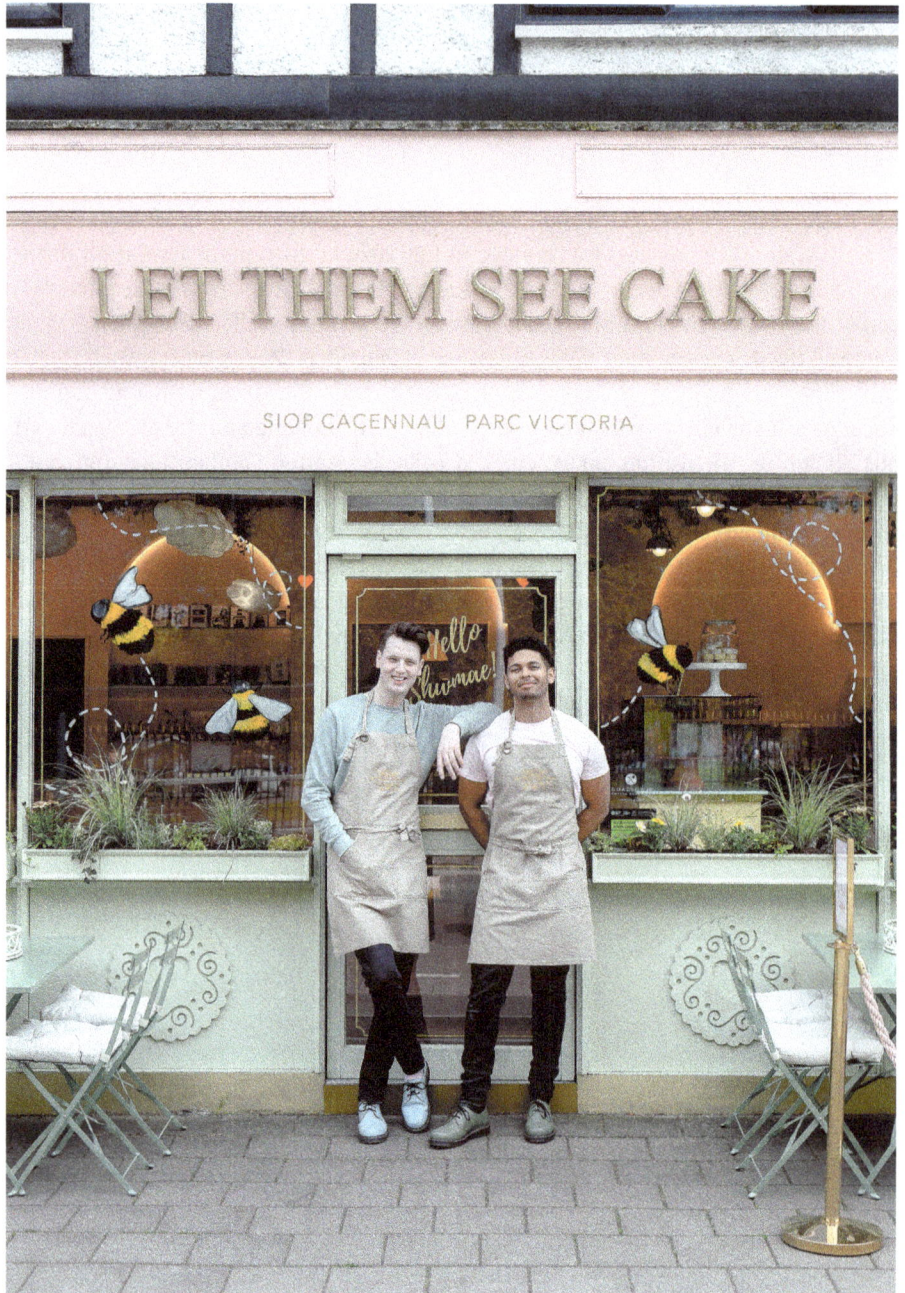

Gareth Davies and Ryan Rowe (Source: Ryan Rowe; photo: Marie Francesca).

Themes

The underlying success of Let Them See Cake is partnership, growing a team together and complete joy in what they do. While the business is a partnership between Gareth and Ryan, the team are an integral part of the family. There are two employees who have been with them from the very beginning, and they have seen them grow in confidence and excel at their skills. The Let Them See Cake philosophy is to have strong individuals come together to make something that amazes their people and brings happiness to everyone who steps into the store.

Let Them See Cake works on respectful, kind, honest and hardworking values, creating an opportunity for people who love cake as much as they do to enter a place that is a little bit different and where they feel they can fit in.

Ryan is the business expert – the buyer, the accountant and the strategist. Gareth is the baker and the team leader. They have a passion for cake but also a responsibility for the people they employ. Gareth feels it is essential to them that the staff enjoy what they are doing:

> it's really important to keep the guys going, making sure that they're all fed and watered, making sure that they're happy. I regularly go around making sure that they're all okay and now again take them for walks to talk about their worries and concerns. We do all have our down days, and because of maybe something outside of work or whatever, I truly feel like they can come to me and talk to me about it, which I think is important in the workplace.

The History

Let Them See Cake is a very entrepreneurial business, having started with small beginnings, then pivoting to new opportunities for the business during the COVID-19 pandemic, and the further growth of the business through developing new products and services. At its heart, Let Them See Cake is a cake business, but has diversified from its initial focus on producing custom-made cakes, to developing cake decorating and sugar work classes, to opening a café in Cardiff with cake delivery services. Gareth Davies began baking cakes with his grandmother while growing up in Aberystwyth, and thought of the idea for Let Them See Cake when he was 16 years old. After attending catering college, Gareth began competing in cake decorating competition after being inspired by a visit to Hotel Olympia in London, where he discovered the creativity of elaborately decorated cakes, to which he said: *'I just thought this is my route.'* At that time, Gareth was scouted for a modelling agency and moved to Cardiff, but continued to hone his craft in cake decorating, winning five gold awards from shows like Cake International in Birmingham and London. Working in modelling gave Gareth a vision for design, taking inspiration from set designs and thinking, *'I wonder if I could do that in cake.'* He started making photos of creating set designs with cakes. Using the resources available around him, he encouraged his model, photographer and make-up friends to help out. At that stage, he worked at the Royal College of Music and Drama in Cardiff and borrowed costumes from the costume lady for his designs, which he sent off to magazines. One made it into a magazine in the USA. Gareth's main design was a ten-tier cake made for St David's Shopping Centre, which he called 'Let Them See Cake,' although at the time he was working under the name Gareth Davies Sugar Craft.

Ryan came on board in 2016–2017, helping out in the evenings and weekends, while working full time in property management. At the beginning, Gareth rented a room and started doing classes on cake making and sugar craft, but they were also selling cakes and created their own website to facilitate the process of people choosing and ordering the cakes that Gareth and Ryan would deliver. With lockdown regulations in place during the COVID-19 pandemic from March 2020, the business was unable to offer classes, therefore when regulations allowed, they focused their attention on cake deliveries, creating treat boxes of various cakes to help people get through the difficulties of lockdown restrictions, where customers would order online and Gareth and Ryan would deliver cake to the customers. During the pandemic, the unit below the apartment where Gareth and Ryan were living at the time became available, and both seized the opportunity to convert the unit into a café, where the business has established themselves ever since. For Gareth, it was a matter of *'we can't miss this opportunity. We need to take this shop.'* More recently, the café has expanded in size to include a larger seating area, moving the cake production to a separate industrial kitchen unit nearby, allowing the business to focus on offering new services, including brunch.

Small Business Enterprise

Cake is the essence of the business, but the business produces a range of cake-related products, from large celebration cakes for special occasions to various cakes on sale in the café, including cupcakes, cookies, macarons and other treats, such as rocky roads, brownies, blondies and doughnuts. Notable for the business are the various flavours of cakes and treats that they produce. Different flavours are available from week to week to provide customers with variety and keep demand higher. Cake flavours can include classic Victoria sponge, lemon and blueberry, chocolate fudge or lemon meringue. Funfetti and Oreo are typical flavours of cupcakes, and macarons typically come in vanilla, chocolate, raspberry or pistachio and cherry flavours. More recently, Let Them See Cake has expanded its offering to include brunches, that include a selection of different French toasts and more savoury items, including eggs, bacon, salmon and potato cakes. With this, the café offers a range of flavoured teas and coffees. The various products that the business has developed since its inception are a sign of the adaptability of the business, and the vision of the entrepreneurs to seek new opportunities. Plans to grow the business include exploring new opportunities to expand the product range and develop new services to expand the reach of the business beyond its current location.

Gareth Davies (Source: Ryan Rowe; photo: Marie Francesca).

Let Them See Cake café (Source: Ryan Rowe; photo: Marie Francesca).

Marketing and Promotional Activities

In terms of marketing, Let Them See Cake is particularly active on social media, and was also featured on the Hot Cakes[1] programme which aired on BBC Wales and BBC Three in 2022. Featured as *'Wales' most Instagramable cake shop,'* this programme brought increased awareness of the business through national exposure on television, expanding the customer base of the business beyond their local area and their initial regulars that have been loyal to the business since the pandemic period. Television exposure has been important for the business, but this coincided with what they describe as the 'Bake Off effect,' in that the general public have become more interested in baking due to the popularity of programmes like *The Great British Bake Off*. This is supplemented by the company's presence on social media, particularly on Instagram and TikTok, as the colourful and visual nature of the business and its products are suited to these platforms, attracting interest from a varied supporter base, possessing over 26,000 followers on Instagram. Their posts underline the creativity of the business, their strong Welsh identity and emphasis on the Welsh language, and they show the personal nature of the business, as many posts revolve around the owners, Gareth and Ryan, as well as the employees of the business. Posts are both informative about the available products and what is on offer at particular times, as well as fun, such as the staff dancing or showing what goes on in making the cakes. Additionally, Let Them See Cake maintains a strong local presence by attending various food festivals and events around Cardiff, such as the Cardiff International Food Festival, and occasionally has pop-up stands in the St David's Shopping Centre in Cardiff city centre. While these are confined to the Cardiff area at present, the owners have expressed their desire to attend events and build their presence further afield.

The Cake Community

As a small business, Let Them See Cake has placed a strong focus on the team behind the business, which aligns with like-minded, creative individuals who have a passion for cake. This is echoed in the vision statement of the company: *'We see our team growing together as one unit, as well as team members growing individually, to make the best experience for us all to keep creating and doing what we love.'* Community is important for business, not just through its staff but also with its customers. As a business located in Wales, there is a strong emphasis on the Welsh language by the entrepreneurs and staff, who mostly speak Welsh. This echoes the community around Victoria Park in Cardiff, where the business is located, as there is a notable community of Welsh speakers in the area. Starting the business during the COVID-19 pandemic, the business developed a loyal customer base in its local area around Victoria Park and the western parts of Car-

---

1 https://www.bbc.co.uk/programmes/p0c1y2bh

diff, as customers were unable to travel very far due to lockdown restrictions. Beginning delivery services enabled the business to expand to other parts of the city, but the customer base has grown much further beyond Cardiff through the company's social media activities, and more significantly from the national exposure that was obtained from the Hot Cakes television programme, drawing attention to the business from across the UK. Attending different food festivals and events has also enabled Let Them See Cake to build a loyal customer base.

Challenges

Since its inception, Let Them See Cake has seen many challenges, none more so than the COVID-19 pandemic, which forced the business to close its original operations of cake decorating and sugar work classes, and pivoting towards cake delivery services and eventually the opening of a café. At the time, this was a risky move as certain lockdown restrictions remained in place, but Gareth and Ryan had the vision to see the growth of the company during this time. The adaptability of being able to develop new activities at this time was important for Let Them See Cake, and this has helped the business to grow since then, leading to the expansion of the seating area in the café, the opening of a new kitchen unit and the move to serving brunches in the café. This flexibility will allow the business to better explore new growth opportunities in future, which the entrepreneurs are actively seeking. This entrepreneurial vision provides the business with better scope for developing resilience during challenging times, and this has been the case since the business has had to meet the challenges of the cost-of-living crisis and periods of economic insecurity from increased costs that have been evident in the post-COVID period in the UK.

The Future

The new café development opened in the summer of 2023 with a popular brunch menu with locally sourced ingredients cooked up into delicious food on the premises. This has resulted in new staff recruitment to cover and fill the skill set required of a brunch chef and front-of-house staff.

Ryan and Gareth continue expanding the business, moving into corporate events which they hope to expand based on the word-of-mouth recommendations and social media campaigns.

The popularity of the café, the pop-up stores and their presence at food festivals had led to customers requesting a home delivery service. While Ryan managed to deliver orders around Cardiff during lockdown, this was reactive rather than strategic and extremely tiring. Working with a team of student entrepreneurs, they are currently looking to open an online shop delivering across the UK.

Bigmoose Coffee Company

Bigmoose Coffee Company is a coffee shop with a heart. They employ, train and mentor people who have experienced homelessness and people who have struggled with their mental health. They work to help the team with their mental health, including providing free therapy, as well as having an open door policy to chat and provide support.

Bigmoose pays staff the real living wage or more and value every single member of staff investing in them all, encouraging them to go on training courses to develop their skills and support them in their personal lives. https://www.bigmoosecoffeecompany.co/coffee-company-info

Synopsis

Bigmoose Coffee Co is a popular cafe in the centre of Cardiff, which has no sign above the door and spends no money on marketing. It serves brunch, sandwiches made from locally baked bread, bagels, homemade pancakes, in-house-baked cakes and sustainably sourced coffees and teas. Bigmoose Coffee Co employs, trains and supports people who have experienced homelessness through a collaboration with Llamau[1] (a youth homeless charity) and other people who are disadvantaged.[2]

In 2014, father and daughter Jeff and Chloe Smith formed a charity in honour of Gary 'Moose' Cloonan, Jeff's ice-hockey player friend who died of cancer. The charity had a plan to help those struggling with their mental health, to prevent suicide and to support those experiencing homelessness.[3] The success of the charity in Cardiff city centre led to the opening of the cafe. At that time, Chloe, a qualified schoolteacher, was 23 years old and looking for a new challenge in life.

---

1 https://www.llamau.org.uk
2 https://www.bigissue.com/news/activism/big-moose-coffee-co-use-power-beans-tackle-homelessness-cardiff/
3 https://www.walesonline.co.uk/news/wales-news/caf-run-dad-daughter-team-23533322

https://doi.org/10.1515/9783110756142-021

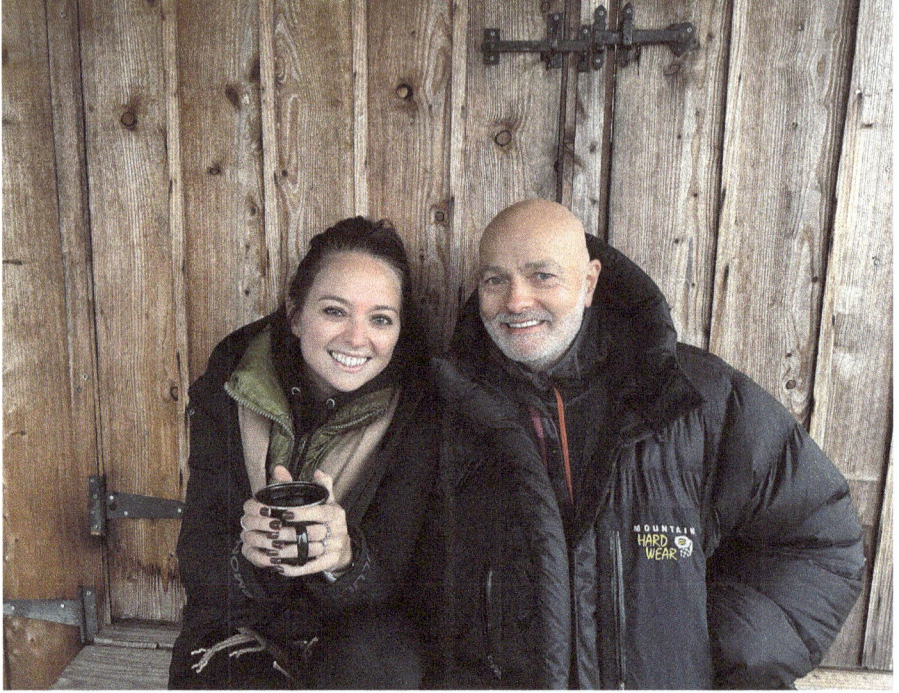

Chloe and Jeff Smith (Source: Alex Jamieson).

History

Jeff and Chloe were inspired to open the coffee shop after volunteering at a local homeless shelter. They launched a Kickstarter campaign that raised over £30,000 to help fund the renovation of a derelict building and the purchase of cafe equipment.

They took on an empty derelict building in the centre of Cardiff, just off a main shopping street, which had been empty and neglected for many years. They renovated the building with the help of a volunteer army of friends and family, including Moose Cloonan's ice-hockey teammates and friends of friends who were skilled tradespeople willing to give their time and expertise for free. The funds raised from the Kickstarter campaign contributed to the cost of raw materials, legal and planning fees, and construction services. Furniture and fittings were sourced from skips outside city-centre retail stores undergoing their own renovations. A retail-store rebrand involves a contractor working out of hours to gut the building and clear the site of unwanted trading counters, flooring, furniture and many other items. Chloe and Jeff collected suitable items discarded by high-street retail brands and upcycled them for the cafe, which is now an exciting, interesting, warm, eclectic space that welcomes everyone.

Big Moose Coffee Café (Source: Alex Jamieson).

Small Business Enterprise

Bigmoose Coffee Co currently employs nineteen local staff, including chefs, baristas and front-of-house staff, with Chloe and Jeff running the charity with three additional employees. They treat everyone as part of the family and provide support and mentor all staff.

The cafe menu has a traditional brunch style, with an emphasis on quality, and offers sandwiches, pasta bakes, grazing plates, cakes and pastries, all freshly made. Local produce is used whenever possible, such as locally roasted coffee. The bread is locally baked, fruit and vegetables are collected from Cardiff Central Market[4] early in the morning; cakes and snacks are baked on the premises. The cafe has a strong moral and altruistic philosophy; however, its success is based on good coffee and good food, without which it would not succeed. Bigmoose Coffee Co is rated the number one coffee shop in Cardiff on TripAdvisor.[5]

The cafe is open to the public every day and also hosts private functions, including birthday parties, wedding receptions and other celebrations. Every private event is tailored to the individual party, resulting in a memorable celebration for all involved. The cafe also hosts 'Life Story' speaker events,[6] tapas evenings and musical nights.

Bigmoose branding uses the logo of a moose with distinctive orange spots, which grabs attention in a crowd and on social media. The company does not pay for marketing or promotion; it relies on word of mouth and social media and the support of events such as the World Homeless Cup 2019 football tournament[7] and the Cardiff Half Marathon. The cafe's location is advertised on a sign on the main road, guiding those who spot it down a side street to the building, which has no signage or branding on the outside.

All profits from the cafe are donated to the Bigmoose Charity which provides mental health support, using the Human Givens approach to therapy.[8] Through the charity, access to this therapy is free to staff, customers and the general public who request help either in person or online.

Challenges

Over the years, Bigmoose Coffee Company has encountered several challenges, which it has worked as a team to overcome. These challenges include the sudden appear-

---

4 https://www.cardiffcouncilproperty.com/cardiff-market/
5 https://www.tripadvisor.com/Restaurant_Review-g186460-d13821431-Reviews-Bigmoose_Coffee_Company-Cardiff_South_Wales_Wales.html
6 https://www.visitcardiff.com/events/bigmoose-life-stories/
7 https://www.homelessworldcup.org/previous-tournaments/cardiff-2019
8 https://www.humangivens.com

ance of a tent city for people experiencing homelessness, when a misconception about the cafe's offering to people who are homeless led to word spreading across the Cardiff homeless community that the side street welcomed rough sleepers. The cafe had to close when the area became unsafe for staff and customers due to drug dealers, violent and aggressive drug users, and inappropriate behaviour, such as using the area outside the cafe as a toilet. Negotiations between homeless charities, people who are homeless and the police resulted in the community moving on after a few months; however, until the situation was resolved, the cafe was unable to trade.

The cafe is often targeted by vandals and thieves, perhaps due to its location on a quiet side street, which is upsetting for staff and customers and causes trading chaos. The cafe recently had two break-ins within the space of three months and posted on social media:

> Once again, we must try to be strong, for our staff, our customers and our community, but [. . .] it's tough and everyone has a tipping point [. . .] Sometimes it's challenging trying to keep positive, but we will, we'll try to keep inspiring and leading our team, and we will never, ever give up! Chloe Smith[9]

This social media post resulted in a demonstration of support from the community, with customers not only raising money to pay for materials but also helping with repairs at the cafe.

The Future

Bigmoose Coffee Company plans to continue to grow the business by expanding into event catering to increase revenue for future growth plans and the development of the charity. Current goals include raising £15 million for the Bigmoose Charity to expand their mental health services with the ultimate aim of saving and changing as many lives as possible.

Chloe is a driven, inspiring, impressive young person, who, with the support of her father and her team, as well as her family, is striving to improve lives in the local community and wider society.

---

9 https://www.walesonline.co.uk/news/wales-news/charity-coffee-shop-cardiff-broken-25833669

Melin Tregwynt

Melin Tregwynt, a small whitewashed woollen mill, can be found in a remote wooded valley on the Pembrokeshire coast.

There has been a mill on this site since the 17th century, when local farmers would bring their fleeces to be spun into yarn and woven into sturdy Welsh wool blankets.

Weathering wars, recessions and the passing of time, the looms have continued to work their magic. Melin Tregwynt fabrics are simple in spirit, satisfying in quality and timeless in design.[1]

Synopsis

Eifion and Amanda Griffiths are the third-generation owners of a small family business in West Wales, based at the furthest point to the West of the UK before you get your feet wet and end up in Ireland. The business was started by Eifion's grandfather in 1912 when there were no cars, no television, no home electricity and no telephone in this remote part of Pembrokeshire. Eifion's grandfather and grandmother arrived at the mill on a horse and cart with all of their furniture on the back of the cart. This is a small business enterprise story about a small family business that, 114 years ago, demonstrated innovation, resilience and the importance of family, and how still do so today.

The mill building has not changed very much at all since the 1930s. There is a perception that it is now a fully automated factor, and it does not remain the tradiional bedrock of the business. Built in the eighteenth century, it was located beside water to allow waterpower to provide energy to run it. At the time, there were eleven mills in Wales using steam power sourced from tiny water streams at time when resources and money were short.

Eifion is a trained, experienced architect who joined the family business in 1981 to help his father run the business. The skills he developed as an architect have contributed to his eye for the design which is essential to the unique selling point of Melin Tregwynt product range. He has an eye for graphics and visuals which are needed for good marketing and social media material, and he has also designed the current mill shop and café.

Amanda is a skilled and experienced accountant who moved naturally from accounting to running the mill. When Eifion's father heard he was to marry a tax consult, he was a little concerned, as time told he did not have to worry as Amanda's accounting and business expertise has contributed significantly to the family business's current prosperity and popularity.

---

1 https://melintregwynt.co.uk/

https://doi.org/10.1515/9783110756142-022

Amanda and Eifion Griffiths (Source: Amanda Griffith).

History

Melin Tregwynt is still the traditional Welsh wool craft mill it was, when Eifion's father bought it in 1912. It continues to manufacture authentic craft traditional Welsh double cloth specialising in hand-woven woollen fabrics and textiles, mainly blankets and throws; in 2023 it marks 114 years since the Griffiths purchased this family business.

The mill was established in 1841 under the name of Dyffryn Bach as part of the Tregwynt Country Estate. When the Griffiths family came to mill in 1912, they renamed it Melin Tregwynt after the valley it is located in.

The Griffith family, headed by Henry, a weaver apprentice born in 1885, married Esther in 1912; just before the wedding, he bought the mill at an auction in Fishguard. Esther had been left a substantial amount of money by her grandfather and they were able to pay £760 for the commercial property. Eifion has the receipt and knows Henry paid a £400 deposit at the auction and the rest in cash on the exchange of contracts.

The textiles produced by the family from 1912 were marketed to the British Army and Welsh coal miners which was a large volume and profitable business; the wool fabric was naturally fire retardant and perfect for uniforms and work overalls. During this period as a working mill in a small rural community, the majority of suppliers and customers were within a very short radius of the mill; farmers would bring their wool to the mill to be processed, and some would be sold back to them for knitting wool and the rest bought from the farmers for weaving into yarn at the mill.

At first the family did not employ anybody else at the mill, they worked at mill and farmed the land across the seasons. Any surplus commercial woollen goods were taken to markets and fairs in and around Fishguard where a barter system was used rather than cash purchases; in 1914 Henry Griffiths sold his motorbike to a local Taylor in the town for his tailoring services, and in 1920 he received a cockerel in part payment for a yard of woollen fabric – all of this activity was written in log books which are still kept in the mill office.

In 1921, a miner's strike in South Wales destroyed the main market for all the woollen mills in Wales. However, World War I resulted in new contracts for mill owners, demanding army blankets, flannel shirts and uniforms. The people living in a remote part of Wales felt able to contribute to the war effort by providing essential woollen products.

During the 1940s and 1950s, many changes occurred, the most significant being the establishment of the Wool Marketing Board[2] established by the Agricultural Marketing Act 1958. The impact of this was that Melin Tregwynt could no longer buy wool directly from a local farmer but had to buy centrally from the British Wool Marketing Board – a fundamental change to the traditional local sourcing of supply chain for every woollen mill in Wales.

In the 1950s, Welsh tourism grew with visitors to West Wales increasing rapidly. Visitors to the mill were keen to buy the products they saw being manufactured. Eifion's father decided to set up a shop in the family home front room. One of Eifion's first child-hood members arrived home from school wondering who on earth, all these strange people were wondering about the family home – they were mill customers. To keep up with consumer demand, Eifion's father built a shop which they still occupy today.

Small Business Enterprise

The mill currently employs 42 people who are not blood relatives but who form a family unit. Their fabrics can be found in all sorts of interesting places, including hotels, television company offices, adverts for unrelated commercial products, charity campaigns and even the Big Brother[3] house.

As a UK manufacturing company trading in an industry in decline, with technology and imports drowning the traditional textile market, this small family business is surviving and thriving in an economy designed to support large businesses, not small family businesses who practice the same production processes as they did over 100 years

---

2 https://www.britishwool.org.uk
3 Cult British reality television show

ago. West Wales is a beautiful and well-visited tourist destination,[4] which, while a lovely and very beautiful holiday location, is very remote with a distinct lack of infrastructure; driving anywhere is a problem due to the narrow lanes with poor access to main roads and motorways. The physical and financial infrastructure of the mill's location in West Wales[5] does not support manufacturing or the growth and development of any small businesses. Trading in a global economy where competition comes not just from a local market, but from other countries who often have modern machinery and significantly lower Labour costs, producing fabrics and textiles significantly cheaper than Melin Tregwynt.

Design – Pattern and Colour

Melin Tregwynt is famous for its range of authentic Welsh double cloth designs weaved in traditional machinery from 100% wool following the same process as over 100 years ago.

Each pattern design is revisable and based on traditional vintage patterns, including Vintage Star, Vintage Rose and St David's Cross. When Eifion joined the business and began to experiment with new patterns and colours, he had an advantage over his father who was colour blind, so he got to choose the colour range of his preference.

Fabric colours are inspired from colours of the seasonal Welsh landscape – the blues of the sea; the greens of the countryside; the pinks and purples of the flowers and fruit growing around the mill.

Commercial Contracts and Collaborations

Melin Tregwnt supplies retail outlets, including John Lewis Partnership, Liberty London and Mucci Japan. Among the designers who have collaborated with Melin Tregwnt are for example Molly Gregory[6] and Paolo Carzana.[7]

Other commercial enterprises include wool items for the new BBC headquarters in Cardiff; the Welsh Millennium Centre; the Victoria and Albert Museum and supply blankets, throws and cushions to luxury hotels, including the St David's Hotel Cardiff, Astoria Hotel, St Petersburg, Tresanton Hotel, Cornwall.[8]

4 https://www.visitpembrokeshire.com/
5 https://www.google.com/maps/place/Melin+Tregwynt/
6 ttps://melintregwynt.co.uk/blogs/projects/molly-gregory
7 https://melintregwynt.co.uk/blogs/projects/paolo-carzana-show
8 https://www.hotel-suppliers.com/wp-content/uploads/2021/05/Melin-Tregwynt-Hotels.pdf

Melin Tregwynt Mill (Source: Amanda Griffith).

A campaign with the food retailer Waitrose[9] was one of the most ambitious commercial projects Eifion and Amanda worked on, and it is likely to have been the most stressful. Waitrose commissioned Melin Tregwynt to produce the world's largest picnic blanket for an advertisement photo shoot in South Africa with a 6-week delivery lead time. *At the time,* the picnic blanket entered the Guinness Book of Records at 40 metres by 44 metres as the world's largest picnic blanket. The stressful element was producing a blanket of this size that could be transported across the world. The blanket was woven in parts, and many rolls of a repeat pattern in the same width were produced to be hand-stitched together on location by Durban sailmakers. Transported to the site, it was then carried up a hill to be rolled down for the World's Largest Picnic. At the end of the project, the huge blanker was deconstructed and taken to local orphanages.

Mill Visitors and Online Customers

Welsh tourism is long established in Pembrokeshire. Melin Tregwynt is a short walk from a spectacular beach, coastal paths and cliff views. It is one of the top tourist attractions in the area where visitors can enter the mill for free and watch fabric weav-

---

9 https://www.waitrose.com/

ing, cutting and sewing of products during the working week, visit the café, frequent the picnic area and visit the mill shop.

The mill shop stands on the same site as that opened by Eifion's father, and it sells blankets, throws, cushions, fashion items and accessories produced in the mill directly to the end consumer. Visitors to the mill shop often become long-term online customers making additional purchases once they arrive home.

A printed catalogue is produced and mailed to those registering at the mill shop and those making online purchases. Having a connection to the product through a visit to the mill has maintained a long-term relationship with customers across the world.

Relationship with Communities

Melin Tregwynt is more than a small rural tourism business. It contributes to the local community in Pembrokeshire, providing a source of stability to the local economy not only through the training and employment of 42 people in a geographically remote and rural area, the sourcing of local produce for the café and tourism but through the support of community projects.

The Melin Tregwynt are members of the Community Foundation in Wales, where projects have included the designing and weaving of a blanket, of which 30% of proceeds go to The Fund for Wales. Store of the Community Fund blanket sold out in the first week and raised over £6000 for the Community Fund for Wales.

Other community activities include the annual Melin Tregwynt Christmas Fayre, where Eifion and Amanda welcome over 50 Welsh and Pembrokeshire artists, crafts makers and bakers to the mill which not only supports Welsh tradespeople but also welcome visitors local and from far afield to the area for a weekend of happiness and joy.

Challenges

COVID-19 and Brexit have challenged many small businesses with changes in supply chains and a shift in the consumer landscape.

Home tourism in the UK increased as COVID-19 restrictions were lifted with government-led initiatives such as Eat Out to Help Out[10] helping small businesses on the road to recovery, including drawing customers to the Mill Café. While not having a huge impact on shop sales at the time, the increase in visitor numbers has led to a broader customer base and increased online shopping.

---

10 https://commonslibrary.parliament.uk/research-briefings/cbp-8978/

Brexit has impacted supplies including the availability and cost of packaging material, an increase in the paperwork and delivery costs of European customer orders and the extraordinary length of time materials and orders are in transit.

Melin Tregwynt traditional weaving (Source: Amanda Griffith).

The Future

Melin Tregwynt is a non-blood-related family business. In its 110th year of trading, the mill transitioned into an employee-owned business which involved setting up an Employee Ownership Trust.[11] While Eifion and Amanda will remain with the business, they have given ownership to the 42 employees who are all part of the Employees Ownership Trust and who have pledged to maintain and promote the traditional weaving skills and knowledge of Eifion's grandfather and father – giving Melin Tregwynt the best possible chance of surviving another 100 years.

Amanda and I inherited the business and have grown it substantially over the last 35 years but now we want to take a step back. It was important for us that Melin Tregwynt remained a viable business and part of its local community, and employee ownership provided the perfect solution for us. We will guide the new management board through the transition, but most importantly the 42-strong workforce will keep their jobs, and skills and knowledge will remain here and be kept alive. We are still very much a family business, just not in blood, but in ethos, belief and tradition. Many employees have worked here for decades, and we even had three generations of one family as part of our team. I am proud to be passing on the company to the new employee board who I know will take the business to new levels of growth. Eifion Griffiths, cited by Bird (2022)

Reference

Bird, J. (2022). Melin Tregwynt marks 110 years with employee ownership deal. https://employeebenefits. co.uk/melin-tregwynt-marks-110-years-with-employee-ownership-deal/

---

11 https://www.bbc.com/news/uk-wales-61081549

Antagrade Electrical

Synopsis

Antagrade was a small family-owned business launched from a kitchen table in 1983 by three friends with some funding from an interested party. It became a fully family-owned run business in 1999. Antagrade is a specialist railway traction power company that became firmly established in 1987 when they won a contract to project manage and install the fixed power supply system and cabling for the London Docklands Light Railway, playing a key role in the development of the tram system, leading to further innovative work on the Manchester Metro Link in 1991.

Antagrade began with James Laidir consulting on a small-scale basis after James returned from working overseas, something he had to do to provide for his family after a period of hardship and financial worries trying to support a wife and seven children.

Driven by the need for family survival, this family business had a different philosophy than the other stories told in this chapter. The constant hard work, lack of rest, lack of self-care or celebration of success, and many of the problems encountered enforced a small family business philosophy of survival for many years.

James Laidir (Source: Carolyn Strong).

https://doi.org/10.1515/9783110756142-023

History

James arrived in the UK from rural Ireland when he was fifteen years old, having left school at a young age due to health issues. He arrived in England with no qualifications and no idea of a potential career. He loved fixing cars with his older brother and developed an interest in engineering. Working as a young apprentice engineer at Switchgear and Cowans, he met his future wife at Park Hospital in Davyhulme (now Trafford General). Margaret was nursing his terminally ill father who took a shine to her – a young Irish nurse who left Dublin alone, aged 20 years old to train as a nurse and later become a district midwife in Manchester.

Antagrade Electrical unequivocally began through the need to pay bills, starting a one-man band growing into a Partnership. After contracting independently for two of James' old colleagues (both called Eric) at Salisbury Engineering, they needed to change their working life; they decided to go into a partnership with James, and they formed a company with no name. After some research, it was discovered that you could select a company name of your choice and pay to register it, alternative you could buy one off the shelf at Company House for (at the time) £5; scrolling through the available names, Antagrade was selected as it meant that the company would always be on the top of an alphabetic list for tenders and other lists. The company was originally backed by Jean Poulson, whom James, Eric and Eric encountered when they worked for Switch Gear and Cowans, an engineering company her father had started and passed on to the family; this initial investment gave them opportunity to tender for national rail traction works and find suitable office space.

James was the Irish hothead who drove the business, and he drove the business hard. Eric and Eric were the engineers and implementers who acted on the strategic plans developed for Antagrade by James. One of the Eric passed away at a very young age, his wife blamed James for driving the business so hard that it made her an early widow – he continued to bring in work in Manchester, the South Coast and London resulting in long working days, travelling and shift work with poor accommodation (they slept in a caravan due to lack of cash flow and funds).

After his death, Eric's family were bought out of the partnership and a new partner joined to oversee the developing rail traction work in London. Ian joined the business, a technical wizard who had worked for General Electric Company since he was 16 years old travelling around South America and Brazil commission railway systems (where he met his wife). Moving back to the UK, he began working on the London Docklands Light Railway, where he met James. Ian started working for Antagrade in August 1987 when they won a new tender to supply further the railway traction installation and maintenance for London Docklands Light Railway. Ian became the only non-blood member of the family business, who was trusted implicitly by James, Matthew and Rebecca. All of the Light Railway work was based in London. James could not leave Cheshire as he had a family of seven children settled at school, his elderly mother close by in

Manchester and financial commitments which would have made this unmanageable. Ian moved to London, where the focus of Antagrade's work was and still is.

The first traction construction worker, Harrold, was appointed shortly after work on the installation of transaction control alongside James, Eric, Eric and Ian. Harrold was the very first employee. There are many funny stories of them working away from home and sharing a caravan. Harrold kept a television on its side so he could lie in bed watching his favourite shows. Long after his retirement, James visited Harrold every Christmas, making a point of taking him to the pub for a pint (even though he did not drink alcohol himself) and giving him Christmas cash bonus.

In 1991, one of James' sons, Matthew, worked long shifts on weekends and during school holidays, digging trenches and installing cables to help deliver contracts. The start of Matthews's commitment to the family business.

During this time, Antagrade employed Margaret, James's wife as a company professional service administrator where she acted as receptionist, administered wages and acted as a bookkeeper. As a nurse, she was qualified to run essential employee first aid courses which reduced company outgoings. Roles (among others) later taken over by one of James' five daughters, Rebecca.

In 1999, Antagrade became a solely family-owned business after an agreement was made in a hospital ward where James was scheduled for major heart surgery. At this point in time, Eric wanted to retire, and Jim was scheduled for major heart surgery. True to his known sense of humour, James made a deal with Eric: if he survived the surgery, he would buy Eric out; if he didn't do well, then obviously, he would not be buying anything. The heart surgery was successful and Antagrade became solely owned by the family, with shares allocated to Margaret and each of James' seven children.

Small Business Enterprise

Antagrade became a fully family-owned business when Matthew joined as a business strategy engineer and Rebecca as a company administrative director. They did not have formal titles but performed these roles among other tasks. Matthew is an engineering graduate and Rebecca is a science graduate with an astute knowledge of traction health and safety; legal contract requirements, accounting and other skills, including excellent client relationship building. Matthew has been involved in the business from digging trenches for the Manchester Metrolink part time as a student to taking on managerial responsibilities to support his father when needed. Applying the knowledge and expertise gained when working for Adidas in The Netherlands and Aramoc in Saudi Arabia, Matthew quickly became a Company Director and Antagrade's Chief Executive Officer.

Rebecca became involved after graduating when James needed a trustworthy and reliable person to do the accounts and wages after a loss of trust in paid employees. A wages employee was caught adding hours to her timesheet and overpaying herself. This led James to be cautious of non-family members controlling accounts, at the time it made good business sense to only employ family in these roles; family can be implicitly trusted. Rebecca rapidly took on more responsibility, running the principal contractor's licence to work on the Network Rail infrastructure, doing audits and accounting tasks, qualifying to do health and safety work and eventually becoming Antagrade Commercial Director.

Antagrade Product/Service

Antagrade is a transport theme company with expertise in railway traction. Matthew equates their role to house building; when you are building a house, there is a team digging the foundations and then screwing in the plug sockets. Antagrade were not part of the Railway Network Gods as James described them. They are the construction team putting it all together being paid a tiny percentage of a massive budget. James was not daft, he knew there was an opportunity to be at the bottom of the pile of the railway construction team. Antagrade never stepped into consultancy at the decision-making level but took advantage of an opportunity to do the essential jobs to implement a massive-scale project.

Such railway traction jobs included London Docklands Light Railway (the first of its kind in the UK); Manchester Metrolink; the East London Line built power system on East London line; numerous Network Rail infrastructure projects and the Channel Tunnel Rail Link enabling project in Ashford London which nearly bankrupt them.

The Channel Tunnel Rail Link was the biggest job they were ever involved in and the one that nearly sent Antagrade bankrupt. The small family business was responsible for overnight shutdowns to install electricity cables for the Channel Tunnel – the tunnel connecting England and France. They ran out of lugs that connect the cables, not having enough of these essential connectors meant that they would not be reopened in time for the morning commuter rush hour; this would incur fines of thousands of pounds per minute, liquated damages which would result in bankruptcy for Antagrade. This was before mobile phones, so James drove to Stafford, where he found a company owner with a warehouse full of these essential parts and drove them to Ashford 'just in time' to avoid bankruptcy.

Manchester Metrolink (Source: GordonBellPhotography / iStock).

Promotional Tactics

So how did a small family-owned business in the North of England get awarded such large contracts with national transport implications? By picking up the phone and talking to people, chasing contacts and leads, charming them and impressing them by delivering contracts and quality work. Word of mouth played a huge part. James had a business instinct but was never a showman, he thank contacts for helping him, for example someone was once very happy with a Tottenham Hotspurs season ticket. The current equivalent of joining *'the right'* golf club to network with the *'right people.'*

Antagrade still has the rudimental brochure and a web page created by Matthew. The contents of this earned Matthew a rollicking from James when they disagreed over the content, a challenge of a father-owned business employing a son.

Challenges

The biggest challenge for James was coping with large projects as a small business with huge responsibility, struggling to maintain a profit to support his family; he did this successfully through the support of long-term contacts who trusted his business expertise.

Matthew worked long working hours with weekend and overnight projects in London, maintaining the Docklands Light Railway and Channel Tunnel Railway Link – lucrative and profitable projects – which led to exhaustion and an impact on family life. He found himself out on railway tracks on a Bank Holiday Monday, walking up and down the railway line fitting cables rather than home with his wife and children. Rebecca worked long office hours in a demanding office environment.

They decided to sell Antagrade, something they had discussed with James before he passed away.

The Future

Antagrade Electrical was bought by an American company; they put a management team in place to run the company, with Matthew and Rebecca remaining as advisors and mentors. All employees were also kept on by the new management company.

James had seven children to provide for, to take on caravan holidays to North Wales for summer vacations. He worked tirelessly to make Antagrade a profitable success with the help of his wife in the early years and two of his children in the later years. He was always very conscious of the company and his personal finances, having nearly lost the family home due to mortgage arrears.

James would be very proud of this outcome. Matthew, Rebecca and the rest of his children have gained financial security from the profitable sale of this small family business which he started at the family's kitchen table. A kitchen table that had his seven children playing under and around as he worked to start the business.

Contributors

Robert Bowen is an International Entrepreneurship Lecturer at Cardiff University, Wales, undertakes research into rural enterprise, regional development and place marketing, with an interest in food and drink SMEs. He has published in various international journals, and presented research at the Welsh Parliament, House of Lords and European Commission. He is currently co-chair of the Rural Enterprise track at the annual Institute of Small Business and Entrepreneurship conference, and Editor of Regions eZine.

Theresa Eriksson is Chief Operating Officer at a Canadian consulting company. She holds a PhD and Master's degree in Informatics.

Andrew Flostrand, PhD is an instructor of business statistics and quantitative analysis at multiple British Columbia post-secondary institutions. He holds an MBA and PhD.

David Kerruish is an innovation and management consultant. He has worked with prominent organisations, including Salesforce, TELUS, Vancity Credit Union and STEMCELL.

Adam J. Mills is Associate Professor of Marketing and Chase Professor of Minority at Loyola University New Orleans College of Business. He serves as Associate Editor of *Journal of Strategic Marketing*, the *International Journal of Advertising* and *Journal of Marketing Education*, as Chair of the American Marketing Association's Marketing Teaching & Learning Group, and sits on the Board of the Marketing Educators' Association. His research investigates the engineering of customer experience, with a focus on branding, service operations and storytelling, and also extends to experiential pedagogy and classroom innovation. His work has been accepted for publication in *Journal of the Academy of Marketing Science, Journal of Business Research, Marketing Theory, Journal of Advertising Research, Journal of Strategic Marketing, Journal of Product and Brand Management, International Journal of Advertising, Journal of Public Affairs, Business Horizons* and *Journal of Marketing Education*. He serves as an Academic Fellow for the Direct Selling Association and a consultant for the Government of Canada's Center for Strategic & International Studies. He was the 2023 recipient of the Federation of Business Disciplines Outstanding Educator Award, the 2020 recipient of the Association of Collegiate Marketing Educators Award for Early Career Excellence in Marketing, the 2019 Journal of Marketing Education Reviewer of the Year, and was awarded the TD Canada Trust Distinguished Teaching Award in 2014.

Christine Pitt, PhD, is an instructor of Entrepreneurship and Business Sustainability at Vancouver Community College. She has published in peer-reviewed journals such as *Business Horizons, Psychology & Marketing, Journal of Business Research* and others.

Anthony Samuel has a PhD from Cardiff University Business School and his multidisciplinary research navigates the complex interfaces between place management/marketing, social enterprises, sustainable business practices and ethical consumption. Anthony is an Associate Editor for *The Journal of Macromarketing*, and his work has been published in a number of leading journals, including *The Journal of Business Ethics, The European Journal of Marketing, Tourism Management, The International Journal of Entrepreneurial Behavior & Research, The Journal of Consumer Behaviour, Local Economy, Computers and Human Behaviour, Technological Forecasting and Social Change, Technovation* and the *Journal of Macromarketing*.

https://doi.org/10.1515/9783110756142-024

Carolyn Strong is a Professor of Marketing at Cardiff Business School. She has published in *Journal of Business Research, Marketing Letters, European Journal of Marketing* and *Journal of Advertising*, among others. She has published an edited collection of ethical and social marketing contributions and is the long-standing Editor-in-Chief of the *Journal of Strategic Marketing*. Her research interests focus on sustainability and the positive contributions marketing can make to society.

Index

https://doi.org/10.1515/9783110756142-025

www.ingramcontent.com/pod-product-compliance
Lightning Source LLC
Chambersburg PA
CBHW081107220326

41598CB00038B/7267